101 Writers' Scene Settings

Unique Location Ideas & Sensory Details for Writers to Create Vivid Scene Settings

Writer's Resource Series

Paula Wynne

Prado Press

London, United Kingdom

Ordering information: Special discounts are available on quantity purchases. For details contact the author via paula@paulawynne.com

First published by Prado Press 2016

24 Caunter Road, Newbury, Berkshire, RG14 1QZ

101 Writers' Scene Settings/ Paula Wynne -- 1st edition
First Published 2016 by Prado Press
ISBN: ISBN-13: 978-1530608492
ISBN-10: 153060849X
Cover Art: Paula Wynne and Kent Wynne
Editor: Betsy Smith

Also by Paula Wynne

Create a Successful Website
Pimp My Site

Writers' Resource Series

Pimp My Fiction
A~Z of Writers' Character Quirks
101 Writers' Scene Settings

Torcal Trilogy

The Grotto's Secret

Grab a Free Copy of Pimp My Fiction

Secrets of writing a successful novel using techniques from the best reference guides on creative writing.

* Improve your writing
* Transform your novel into a page-turning best seller
* Ensure your success as a novelist

Pick up your free copy: http://eepurl.com/bC336f

Dedication

To novelists who write about locations so their readers can go to special, magical places that seep into them, capture their imagination, and make them remember that setting long after they have left.

"The writer operates at a peculiar crossroads where time and place and eternity somehow meet. His problem is to find that location."

Flannery O'Connor

Foreword

One of the most overlooked elements in first novels by authors is setting. Often setting is thought of as boring or something a writer should "hurry up and get done with" in order to move to the "real story"—the plot of the novel or purpose of a scene.

But setting is not only essential for transporting the reader into the world of story; it's necessary to bring cohesion to a scene's unfolding. If a reader doesn't know where the characters are or what it looks and feels like, she might get confused or stop reading.

As a professional writing coach, I critique more than two hundred manuscripts a year, and many (perhaps most) of those are strongly lacking in setting. I'm often asking, "Where does this scene take place?" and "What does the scenery look and smell and feel like?" Settings evoke moods and can be used powerfully in novels to reveal character and complicate plot developments.

So 101 Writers' Scene Settings is a welcome addition to the resource shelf for writers. Paula Wynne takes special care in this book to explore a wide variety of setting possibilities for scenes, some of which include settings based on the type of terrain or scenery as well as unique aspects to a setting (tight and narrow places, for example).

Reading about these different types of settings can spark ideas and help writers envision and get a sense of places they've never been.

Paula gives tips on what elements should be included when describing settings (mood, colours, weather) and the kinds of physical details one might notice.

Also important are the backstory, genre, and character history and personality that might be impacted or impact a particular setting.

With each setting listing, Paula suggests general, mood, and item details. These very specific locations with their own unique stories and histories help writers to not just immerse themselves in the places she suggests but also to envision similar settings of their own that will be just right for their story.

While there are of course thousands of other potential settings for story scenes, 101 Writers' Scene Settings provides plenty of creative, unique places that will undoubtedly give writers all they need to create sensory-rich settings. Put this book on a special place on your shelf—near your desk so you can refer to it often!

C. S. Lakin, author of The Writer's Toolbox Series

Contents

Introduction

"We're not lost. We're locationally challenged."
John M. Ford

Scene settings are critical pieces of the puzzle that will eventually make up your entire novel.

It might be new novel settings that you require, or maybe you need to vamp up current scene locations that are not fitting snugly into the rest of your plot.

Most of the time, writers and authors use locales that they know, so their scene settings naturally come with a sense of familiarity and comfort. But what about exciting readers with new places for them to experience through the characters? After all, the reason readers read is to travel to new places, meet new people, and experience new emotions—all through the stories created in someone else's mind.

As writers we are taught that everything in our scenes must be seen through the eyes of our POV characters. This is vitally important when looking at your novel's scene settings. Your hero may love a certain place, but someone else, possibly your villain, will hate it. You may experience that same love/hate experience as you browse through this list of settings ideas. More importantly, *101 Writers' Scene Settings* is aimed at helping you to determine whether a particular setting may work for your story, or perhaps it may inspire some new ideas of your own.

Don't Just Write a Scene—Create a Memorable Setting

Make your novel's scene settings come alive to your readers with mood, senses, atmosphere, and vivid descriptions shown through the point of view of your characters. This book will guide you through choosing settings with mood, atmosphere, and sensory details that will influence your characters.

In films that feature characters like Jason Bourne or James Bond, you see baddies chasing the hero through crowded towns with tight corners and narrow streets, or racing across rooftops. In other classic films you may see the most unusual places on earth and wonder how the studios found those places to feature in their films.

Many have unrestricted budgets and numerous bodies to act as scouts for locations. But what if there was a resource that writers could dip in and out of to find these special types of locations for setting their scenes?

101 Writers' Scene Settings will guide you through

- creating a novel setting in order to write a vivid scene.
- finding unique locations for different scenarios in your plot.
- creating vivid descriptions for your scene setting, and weaving them together seamlessly through the characters' actions and reactions.
- developing all the elements within a location to ensure you write realistic, intriguing descriptions shown from your character's point of view
- using sensory details that bring your setting to life.
- creating layers of details that make readers feel as though they are right there with your character.

To make your search even more convenient, you will get a free download copy of the Settings Checklist!

Filled with categories of ideas for settings such as crowded towns, tight and narrow streets, adventure-filled locations, places up high and down low, mountains and valleys, seascapes, abandoned places, modern techno settings, scary and spooky environments, and unusual work places, homes, and gathering places, *101 Writers' Scene Settings* helps you to dive into the researching and planning of your settings so that you can easily put together a compelling scene and create a vivid setting that readers won't forget.

This book also includes expert scene setting advice from such successful authors as Linda Abbott, Steve Alcorn, James Becker, Glenn Cooper, Jeff Gerke, Angela Marsons, C. S. Lakin, Marti Leimbach, Rayne Hall, Alex Myers, Jodie Renner, Douglas E. Richards, and Joyce Schneider.

Using *101 Writers' Scene Settings*

First you'll find a list of categories, which of course is only my list; you will no doubt have stacks of different ideas. So scribble those down among mine.

I added some interesting facts from my Scenes Checklist before I started searching for amazing settings. Download your copy now at http://eepurl.com/bC_vjX; you'll be added to my mailing list to receive any future updates.

Even if you don't want to use the exact information included with the settings I have listed, the vivid details I have included are meant to inspire you to create your own places.

You can also mix and match to make up a new place. For example, you may want a place in the mountains with a hot climate, but you see a stunning location in the list that is wintery. No problem.

Just imagine how that place could suit your story, and change it according to your plot threads. When you're done, make up a name for your new setting. You may even fancy combining three locations into one by taking certain elements from all three and making up your own setting.

Adding layers is easy. If you find a place that looks sunny and bright, but you want it dark and foreboding in your scene, just add an imagined layer of gloomy clouds and shadows. In an instant you have a scary setting in the location you want.

Or vice versa—if you find a location that is listed as romantic or spooky, but you want it for your children's book, simply change the elements to suit your plot and characters. Any of the listed settings could be used for a children's book or young adult novel. The same goes for genres. Although I do suggest genres I think the setting would suit, don't limit your imagination. If you see a setting that seems ideal for your genre, use it. Change and modify as you need, or let it inspire you to create your own fictional setting with any or all of that particular setting's elements.

It's great fun and will ensure that your creative juices are flowing when you get to that point in your story when you have to place your characters into your scene. (Don't miss out on learning how to create characters from the list of resource guides in *Pimp My Fiction*.)

If you download the free templates (in this book and *Pimp My Fiction*) and stay on my mailing list, you will be given the opportunity to get a free review copy of my next books, which include an *Indie Author Guide to Book Marketing*, with 100s of ways to promote your book, as well as other books for writers.

Settings Checklist

"An author knows his landscape best; he can stand around, smell the wind, get a feel for his place."

Tony Hillerman

As writers we are taught that everything in our scenes must be seen through the eyes of our POV characters. This is vitally important when looking at the scene settings. Your hero may love a certain place, but someone else, possibly your villain, will hate it. Or vice versa.

When you read Rayne Hall's book called *Writing Vivid Settings*, you will see her illustrations of how powerful this is when showing a scene through different people's eyes. Rayne gives an example of how one setting can change. She takes a kitchen, and then shows how different characters would see that kitchen.

Depending on who they are, what they do, and their background, that kitchen is a completely different place to each of them. That's why it's important to *know* your characters so that *they* can experience the setting, not *you*, the author. I was staggered to see how differently a kitchen can be perceived through the eyes of a handful of different characters.

The same will happen here. I have listed some very basic thoughts and ideas designed to generate deeper opinions from you, whether that particular setting may work for your story, or if it inspires something else in you.

Please feel free to scribble your own notes all over this book. I won't be offended. In fact, I will be delighted because I know it is working and triggering ideas for you to bounce around. I have a huge collection of writing books, and my most treasured have sticky post-it notes sticking out everywhere, all of them covered in pencil scribbles. I firmly believe that those authors would be delighted to know their book inspired so many ideas spilling over onto their pages.

If you experience positive or negative feelings about a listed setting, write down any good or bad things as they come to you for future use. You could note down what a hero or villain would feel about the place to use for whoever's point of view you are writing.

There are so many more categories you will probably jot down as you read mine; I have scribbled a note beside each one to inspire you to find different settings under each category.

Later on I will save you lots of typing time and give you a link to download this Settings Checklist!

Setting Categories

1. Crowded Towns: places with narrow streets and crowded markets and roof top chases
2. Tight and Narrow: for placing the hero in a tight spot where he has to work out how to get out
3. Wide Open Spaces: get lost in some forests and canyons
4. Adventurous: treacherous locations where adventurous heroes climb formidable cliffs or villains chase heroes through rainforests
5. Up High: risky scene settings way up
6. Down Below: delve underground into tunnels and caves
7. Modern Techno: space age buildings or futuristic designs
8. Historical: ancient places with history
9. Seascapes: lighthouse or sunken ship or home jutting out from the edge of cliff

10. Mountains and Valleys: exceptional mountains or winding valleys where the villain can chase the hero

11. Scary and Spooky: mansions, castles, underground railways, whatever will terrify a reader

12. Abandoned: buildings, homes or entire villages

13. Country Life: peaceful meadows with lambs, or wild and rugged wheat fields where murders can take place

14. Unusual Homes: weird, way-out or simply horrid homes where heroes or villains live, such as a lighthouse, boat house or world war bunker

15. Unusual Offices: places or buildings or areas where characters could work

16. Unusual Fight Scenes: places where the villain and hero clash

17. Unusual Love Scenes: where lovers could unite

I originally had a category called 'Family Friendly: Places you could take the kids or even places you wouldn't dare take the them.' But as I wrote up the lists, I added that as an item of detail under each setting.

So if you're writing a family adventure or drama, luckily for you, each listing mentions whether it is family friendly or not, and why.

Of course, the list of possible scene settings is endless. As you browse through my short list, why not add all of the possible settings that spring into your mind? That way you can start to create your own resource file of settings for future writing projects. Here are a few suggestions for the details to include in your listings:

Setting Details

Title: Give each listing a creative title.

Name: Create a specific name.

Geographical Area: Note the town and country, even if you intend to make up a fictional place instead.

USP: List anything that's unique about this place and why or how it could be used in a story setting.

Brief Description: Give a vivid description about this place in a sentence or two. Also make notes of any facts that may be of interest to your story later on. Possibly mention when the place was built or how it came into existence. These types of notes could be important to your story when you're in the writing process.

Mood Details

Mood: Define the mood you feel when you set eyes on this place.

Colours: Identify the colours that stand out. This could be anything from water or greenery to the daylight or sunset colours. It could also be a dominant colour that strikes you the first time you see an image of the place. Note down any feelings and what you think the atmosphere would be like from the colour.

Weather: Make brief or detailed notes on the kind of weather this place would experience and how it could affect your plot points. Will this weather cause delays and dampen the hero's mood? You may also want to set a reminder to yourself about the kind of mood the weather could give your character and how you will *show* this through your character's eyes. For example, if a place is dark and gloomy, it could be eerie and spooky for your heroine. Maybe this type of weather will play a big role in disrupting all your hero's plans.

In her book *Captivate Your Reader*, Jodie Renner says: 'Use weather wisely. Let it affect your characters' moods and behavior. Let it impact the plot and create complications.'

Visual: Mention a small visual detail, either one or two, that strikes you first when looking at this place. It could be something specific which stands out or a distinguishing feature of the place.

Item Details

Ground: A brief description of the ground or, if it's an interior place, what the flooring or carpet is like. This will help when your character has to creep, crawl, march, sneak or bolt across the ground or floor of this place, and you'll know what kind of sound it will make.

Ceiling: A brief creative description of the ceiling or sky. Again to remind you of how it will be viewed through your POV's eyes.

Walls: This is important for adding in little sensory details (coming next) about the place. If the walls in a ruin are stone and crumbly, or slippery and mouldy, it will affect your character's sense of touch. If there are no walls, then it could be wide open to the elements. Again, that could add depth to your setting and show your hero's emotional state.

Doors: Unless it's an open-space design, almost every building or room has an entrance door. Make a note of what each door looks like. How does it sound when it opens? How does it sound when it closes? This is great for weaving sensory details into your scene: the character doesn't just open a spooky looking, decaying door; it will creak open or be almost falling off rusty hinges. I'm currently reading *Shoot Your Novel* by CS Lakin to learn more about writing cinematically to ensure I never deviate from creating real-life scenes for my readers.

Although I am only into the first few chapters, already my mind is thinking like a movie director and looking at different aspects of a setting, such as how my character will enter this place: climb in, sneak under, crash the door down, or not go in at all, but peep inside to spy on the occupants. I will give a review on this book (and any others) in the updated version of *Pimp My Fiction*, which you'll get free if you download my Scenes Checklist in the last chapter of this book.

Props: I learnt a lot about props from Rayne Hall's book on writing fight scenes. I love how Rayne makes a writer 'see' a setting and find objects, items and props scattered around that a hero would come across. These props could be used for symbolism to enhance your setting, and to show the character in action moving through the place.

The same props can also be perfect for a natural fight scene. Don't let your baddies pull out a gun. That's lazy, unless they're obsessed with guns. Instead, use the props as weapons. I did this in my novel *The Grotto's Secret,* and one of my beta readers told me the baddie was disgusting because of what he did to another character using natural props in the setting. I was thrilled that my baddie had created such a strong emotional response in this reader.

Obstacles: Like the props mentioned above, list any obstacles that could trip up a hero, set him off balance or be used by the villain against him. This can be anything from the props, to the ceiling, walls, doors, weather, or other people. Absolutely anything.

These notes will definitely help you when you're writing up the scene, and they'll act as triggers to make you think of all kinds of 'stones' you can throw at your characters to keep giving them challenges.

Plants: This could be another obstacle if the plants are dense vegetation or thorny brambles that prevent the hero from getting in or out of the setting. It could show the state of the place; for example, a bright and breezy room lovingly decorated with flowers could be the setting for a romance. Note any plant life that you could use, even if you think you won't at least it's there in your notes if you change your mind.

Animals: Animals in a scene consist of anything from spiders in a web that your character walks into in a dark tunnel to rats scuttling around in the dark. Many authors use sensory details such as the sound of an owl hooting in the distant tree tops. All these little things make your scene real to the reader.

So note down any animals or insects that could inhabit this place, from spiders and snakes and creepy crawlies, to pets and wildlife, or monsters and dragons that you'll have roaming around your setting. They're all important background details that will bring your setting to life. Often animals *are* the story, as they were in Jurassic Park; in other cases, they play a major role, especially in fantasy or science fiction tales.

General Details

Backstory: Here you'll make any interesting notes or historical facts that make the place special or that will enhance your story.

For example, there may have been a natural disaster in the area or close by that could later come into play, or a historic event that could affect your hero and upset the apple cart. Basic or detailed, keep the notes in case you want to refer to them later on.

Genre or Scene Type: You may only write one genre, which is fine, but you could add random thoughts on what type of scene would be ideal for this setting, such as a love scene, fight scene, or car chase. Also, note any other genres in case one day you want to delve into a new genre, and then you'll see at a quick glance where your storyline could go, anything along the lines of thriller, mystery, romance, children's, horror, etc.

People Details

People: Write down what kind of people live or work or come to this place. If it's a historical setting, mention their clothing and what type of people they are: committed to family and community, or loners. Be specific with vibrant details, yet don't forget that readers read to imagine things too, so don't over-write. Give them some relevant and specific details and then let their imagination do the rest.

Family or non-family friendly: Would you take kids or the old folks there?

Sensory Details

Light up your setting by evoking as many of the senses as possible.

If you need help on this topic, I strongly recommend Jodie Renner's book *Captivate Your Reader*. She has a chapter dedicated to how to use sensory descriptors. She says: 'Zoom in on some telling details, like smudges on a mirror, sweat on a brow, condensation on a glass, steam from a coffee cup, fists clenched, hands shaking, shoulders hunched, etc.'

Sights: What will your hero notice straight away or when he takes a closer look? Note any overwhelming sights or noticeable things about the place, and maybe a one-liner to remind you of your immediate feelings when looking at it. This is where your colours will come in as well, so you can refer to the item details you wrote down earlier. Write up a detailed description, but remember to only spread the most important aspects through your scene.

Smells: What scents, perfumes, tangs or odours would your character smell? You may want to write down good and bad smells because you can use both, depending on who is smelling the things. For example, fish or seafood can be disgusting to someone who hates fish, yet it smells delish to someone who can't get enough of it.

Think of the smell of baking bread that lures you towards it whenever you enter a supermarket or shopping mall. Or the rich aroma of freshly brewed coffee. And then use memories or moments from the heroine's past that could add depth to the setting.

In *The Grotto's Secret*, my modern-day heroine's mother had died at a young age, and whenever my heroine walked into a kitchen she could smell her mother's apple pie baking, even when she was in the kitchen of a derelict mansion.

Memories show a character's backstory or hurts and tragedies, as well as happy, fond recollections. If you're writing a crime, find out what dead bodies smell like so your character can react to that odour. If she works in an unusual place, show smells through the character's senses.

Taste: Make notes of any possible tastes that a hero may experience, like eating stale, sour bread because he's starving, or drinking bitter lemons when he's ill. Characters don't have to be sitting down to dinner to use their sense of taste. Tastes can be woven into the initial description of the scene, or better still, while a character is moving through the setting.

Touch: Describe what some things from this place would feel like. Use touch descriptors like sticky and clammy, slimy or slippery, rough or smooth. Even when a character is in full action - like running away from the villain - drop in that her hand scrapes along a rough wall, or she picks up a smooth, cold broken mirror to defend herself. If she's having a meal in a sleazy pub, describe the oily feeling of grease on her hands.

Sounds: Describe what sounds your POV character would hear in this setting. These could be good or bad sounds, depending on the point of view of your character. For example, a wind chime may sound melodious and calming to one person, but downright irritating to another. Sounds are probably the easiest way to draw your reader into the scene and establish an emotional connection.

For example, in a scary scene the door or floorboards creaking, or footsteps crunching on gravel, or a thump and heavy breathing near where the heroine is hiding will make your reader feel scared, too. Likewise, happy and fun sounds in your romance will lift the reader's mood. Read *Writing for Emotional Impact* by Karl Iglesias to see how you can ensure that the reader experiences the same emotional journey as your characters.

Character's Personal Details

I am mentioning this here, but I haven't listed this in any of my examples in this book. That's because these details are based solely on your characters and what their emotional state is at any given point in your story.

When you are going through my list and scribbling notes like mad as you get inspired by the settings, make a list of the following items because only *you* know who your characters are and what they're feeling when they're in that particular place.

Objectives, Secret Revelations, Obstacles and Disasters In my Scenes Checklist (find the link in the last chapter) you'll see that each scene must have objectives for your POV character: a possible secret revelation, an obstacle he must overcome to move to the next scene, or a disaster, which is not necessarily a major catastrophe, but something that must happen so your character is in a worse position at the end of the scene. This will make your reader read on.

So when you like a setting, make some notes about a possible objective for your hero, what could be revealed here, the obstacles he will overcome—both emotionally and physically — and how this setting could create a disaster or bad outcome for your character.

Emotions Make notes of how your POV character could be feeling in this setting. This will depend entirely on how you have created your character, what flaws she has, and what has hurt her in the past or made her happy.

If you don't have a copy of *The Emotion Thesaurus* by Angela Ackerman and Becca Puglisi, do yourself a favour and get one now. It is one of the best resources a writer can have. It lists all emotions and explains how to 'show' emotions and not tell your reader what that character is feeling. You simply have to have a copy beside you at all times when you're writing your story!

High Moment In her book *The 12 Pillars of Novel Construction*, Susanne Lakin tells you to choose the best place for your scene's high moment.

Susanne says: 'Whether setting is a huge element in your story because of your premise or not, you can make setting powerful and impacting by choosing each place carefully.' So, make notes here about possible places within this setting where you could stage your high moment and why.

Susanne advocates that, in every scene, we must consider our character's high moment and the plot point we are going to reveal. We must work out the dynamics and conflict of the characters in that scene so that we can place our characters strategically to generate the most conflict (inner and outer) and the strongest emotions.

For this part of your setting notes, think about what you've planted into the POV character's past and how those things can connect to this setting. If nothing comes to you at this point, don't worry; just continue with your setting notes and come back to it when it pours out of your bubbling pot.

Emotional Connection to Setting You may want to follow more of Susanne's advice and have your character visit a place that holds powerful memories of their parent, past, or any other memorable events, either positive or negative, or both. Those emotions can drive a scene, and the memories triggered there can induce conflict.

So use a setting from a character's past, and then when she visits it now as a 'connected setting' in your current scene, it will trigger emotions. This will create the strongest impact for your scene.

In her book *The Heart of Your Story*, Susanne tells us to choose settings that will stir memories. Think of places that will allow your character's emotions, needs, dreams and fears to rise to the surface.

Susanne says, 'Put your characters in a place on purpose. Stop and think before you create a scene. Where is the best place to put your character to lead to an important moment in the scene? Deliberately choose a setting that will best serve the interests of your plot and your character's need for that scene and you will have a much more powerful novel.'

Take a look at Susanne's long checklist in *The Heart of Your Story* to find out what to ask your characters about the setting they find themselves in. Knowing this kind of information is vital to making the setting come alive for your character, therefore making it come alive for your reader as well. Susanne has also kindly shared this link for her Scene Structure Checklist: http://bit.ly/1yQEu43

Symbols Symbols have a physical presence in your story. They lend implied meaning to the characters, places or events that surround them. They can be images, ideas, sounds or words that embody a theme.

In her book *Writing Vivid Settings*, Rayne also suggests the use of symbols to bring your setting to life. Rayne says: 'Here's a trick for giving your novel a subtle literary touch: symbolism. When something in the setting reflects something of the story's deeper meaning, it becomes a symbol. This is useful if you want your readers to get a lasting impression of your book, not just momentary entertainment. Symbolism is an advanced technique. Skilled writers can use it deftly, but if you're new to fiction writing, it's best to apply it with a light brush.'

You may want to try Rayne's two approaches and see which of them suits you best:

1. Consider your novel's theme and create symbols to reflect it.

2. Consider the types of setting in your novel, and use them as symbols.

Steve Alcorn also tells us about symbolism in his book *How to Fix Your Novel*: 'To be effective, a symbol needs to relate to something important in your story: a character, a setting, or perhaps the story's theme itself. By looking for potential symbols before you start writing your novel, you can add depth and complexity to your work.'

Motifs Like symbols, motifs can also be images, ideas, sounds or words, but they will be a recurring element that adds meaning to the story. Motifs can establish mood and atmosphere (see Mood Details) and show symbolic themes within your story.

What's the difference between a Motif and a Symbol? They are similar, so it's confusing to know which is which. The main difference between motifs and symbols is the element of repetition.

Motif A distinctive feature or repeating idea. Its meaning depends on how you use it in your story. It contributes towards story and theme development.

Symbol An object, emblem, token, or sign signifying something deeper and more important. Its meaning can be defined by its history and purpose. It may appear in a particular setting or scene, or a couple of times in a story.

Before you finish making notes on any of the settings I have listed that may trigger some thoughts or inspire your character to pop into that setting, think about any symbols and motifs in that setting that may give your character and reader an emotional link to the place.

You may want to start with the props or obstacles I have listed. Find images, ideas, sounds, words, objects, emblems, tokens, or signs that will mean something to your character.

Better still, search deep inside your character and their story to find something suitable that will offer implicit significance to the characters and settings where your plot and story unfold.

Similes and Metaphors A metaphor is a figure of speech that recognises something as corresponding to another unrelated item to suggest similarities between the two. Whereas a simile also compares two different things, but with the use of *as* or *like*. Using similes and metaphors is an effective way to make a description more vivid and interesting.

In his book *How to Fix Your Novel,* Steve Alcorn says: 'Metaphors play an important role in fiction. They turn everyday writing into a sparkling gem that makes us pause and appreciate its beauty. But in addition to delighting us, a great metaphor can help us better understand the meaning behind the words. Some metaphors and similes are simply beautiful ways to create vivid descriptions, while others are almost laugh-out-loud funny and can really bring your writing to life.'

Here are some of Steve's favourite metaphors and similes that liven up a setting:

From Scott Westerfeld's *The Last Days*: 'Pearl's room looked like a recording studio had mated with a junkyard, then exploded.'

From Markus Zusak's *The Book Thief*: 'The plane was still coughing. Smoke leaking out from both its lungs.'

And: 'The streets were ruptured veins.'

And: 'Trees wore blankets of ice.'

The last example from Markus could be both metaphors and personification. See notes on this coming up.

In Rayne Hall's book *Writing Vivid Settings,* she advocates that using a simile in your description is a 'powerful method, because it accomplishes more than just a description. If done well, it reveals something about the POV character's world. Good similes are original, creative, clever, and sometimes funny.'

Rayne gives these examples:

'The thunder sounded like a giant ripping sheet.'

'The sky looked grey like bed sheets that had been boil-washed with dirty socks.'

'The storm sounded as if someone was slapping wet sheets against the wall.'

She advises: 'Choose something from within the novel's world. This strengthens the world-building, giving the reader additional rich information about that world, its period, and its attitudes. If possible, choose something that's specific to your POV' character's experience. When your character encounters something unfamiliar, compare it with something that's familiar to him. This tells the reader a lot about the character's thought processes and background. This can work well to reveal backstory.'

Here are a couple of Rayne's examples that reveal something about social background and family:

'... as big as her parents' tennis court.'

'... smelled like the dormitory at the orphanage.'

So, at this point in your setting brief, worm yourself back into your character's mind and jot down any similes or metaphors with their perception of the setting.

Personification: Because personification is giving human qualities to an inanimate object or an animal, it's another great way to add interest to your setting. Although it's somewhat different from a metaphor, it's still similar in that it increases vividness by bringing inanimate things to life.

When you're documenting your setting notes from your characters' perspectives, keep in mind that they may see an object or item completely different from what you or another character might see. For example, one character may fear the weather and thus hear 'thunder grumble' or the 'wind howl its objection.' From another fictional person's POV it could be that the 'thunder grumbles like their granddad,' giving them fond memories of someone in their family.

Personification is another writing technique that can be used to set the mood. In *The Grotto's Secret*, my modern character is having a tough time and comes home with the 'wind growling in behind her,' thus setting up something horrible about to happen to her.

Here's another phrase I used in *The Grotto's Secret* when my medieval character also comes home to find something wrong: 'the shadows threw their long gnarled fingers across her thatched roof.'

These two characters' stories run parallel to each other, and I was thrilled to have one of my beta readers say, 'Past and present blended masterfully together in this page-turning historical conspiracy thriller guaranteed to leave readers wanting more.'

Alternatively, personification can set a fun, happy mood through something like 'The bees played hide and seek with the flowers' or a bit of humour by having 'The raindrops report for duty.'

If you need inspiration, try Googling some examples of personification and then, bearing in mind your character's emotional state, twist those models around into your own original ideas straight from your character's perspective. The more you get to know your hero or heroine, the more their own original thoughts and feelings will come to you, along with metaphors or similes and personification ideas from their point of view.

Remember, too, that at different points in the story a character may see the weather or one of the setting props in completely different ways. Weave personification into your setting where possible to bring the inanimate objects around your character to life.

Now Your Turn

Go through the list I have created for you. Note down anything that inspires you. Maybe a character pops into your mind. Or a plot thread. Add any other details you can think of, especially sensory details.

I have given you one full example of the details above for each of my categories. After you go through them, copy the Settings Checklist and start making your own notes on the scene descriptions I have listed. If you would like to have a copy of the Settings Checklist in a Word document, I have provided a link at the end of this book to download my version. Save it and make up your own notes for anything more that comes to you. If you want to share that with me, I will be delighted and can even add it to future updates of this book, with you credited as the contributor.

Another way to contribute: if you know of any other settings that should be listed here, please drop me a line and I will include them in the future book updates, with you as the contributor.

Weave The Details

If you've read *Pimp My Fiction*, and in particular the chapter on creating vivid settings, you will remember that the advice those fantastic writing tutors gave was to spread the details throughout your scene and not to dump it all in one place.

Imagine you are threading gorgeous, glittery beads through a jersey dress or top for an evening out. You wouldn't just pile them on top of one another or sew them all across the first place you start. You would find different spots where the beads would shine the brightest and you'd carefully thread them into those special places.

You'll be doing much the same for the information you gather for your settings.

When you're writing your scene, be sure to keep thinking of your beaded outfit. The dress would be your long scene and a top is a shorter scene. Just like the beads are vital to make your ensemble stand out at your event, so too are the details you thread throughout your scene.

It's also important to put your setting details into action. Rather than just 'telling' your reader about them, show what your characters do with those details, and what they touch, feel, hear, see, and smell. Don't force your readers to skip over long sentences of description; embed it so skillfully through the action taking place that they won't even notice you have given them a detailed description.

More importantly, we learnt the importance of showing the setting details through the character's POV, how *the character* would see, hear, and feel everything in that place, not *you*. Give your readers a sensory experience. Don't tell them what the weather is like, show how your character is sweating or how the soft rain glistens on their cheeks.

In *The Grotto's Secret*, I did my research on the medieval settings and then info dumped on my first draft. During the many rewrites, I kept looking for places throughout the scene where I could place those details so that the scene seemed real and natural.

In the end the scenes came alive and I was thrilled when my beta readers told me they could 'see' the scenes cinematically, just as in a movie.

One last thing before we go searching for unique settings: I read in one of my treasured resource guides that you should think of your setting as a stage. That stage will show your readers where in the world the character is (geographically), what's happening with the weather, and what time it is. Then turn your characters loose onto the stage with the settings checklist.

Whether you want your protagonist and villain charging around a hospital, a cinema, a supermarket, or a bus station, or chasing each other through forests, offices, or even a church, any of the settings I have listed will give you the inspiration to create vivid settings that will hook your readers and keep them turning the pages.

Pimp My Fiction also gives you excellent books to read on how to use descriptions. (By the way, I haven't been referring to *Pimp My Fiction* so that you buy my book; remember, I have given you a free download at the beginning of this book.)

Now, enough of my babble, let's go explore some amazing location settings ...

Abandoned

Buildings, homes or entire villages left to rot in the elements.

Bombed Out

Name: Agdam

Geographical Area: Azerbaijan

Brief Description: The forces of the Nagorno-Karabakh Republic captured Agdam during their 1993 offensive. The heavy fighting forced the entire population to flee. After they took possession of the town, the Armenian forces of Nagorno-Karabkh decided to destroy much of Agdam to discourage the Azerbaijanis from recapturing it.

USP: Maybe your action hero or spy thriller heroine came here during the war and now wants to bring the town back to life. Or maybe you'll set your story during the war, showing him rescuing civilians and removing them to safety. Does he get shot in the end?

Mood Details

Mood: Sad and lonely.

Colours: Blood red, olive green and decaying brown are the predominant colours showing the sadness in this village.

Weather: Continental, with an average temperature of 12°C.

Visual: The town's large Agdam Mosque survives intact, even though it's in derelict condition.

Item Details

Ground: Soil and asphalt in some parts, grassy banks where bloodied bodies once lay.

Ceiling: Most rooftops have collapsed over time. The ones remaining in parts have been taken over by wild bushes and weeds.

Walls: Most walls are made of stone and in poor condition.

Doors: Most doors were destroyed; the mosque had a wooden frame, which once glowed with light coming through the glass.

Props: Abandoned belongings of the community such as dolls, clothes and food.

Obstacles: Unstable buildings, some could collapse at any time, few locations to use as shelter because they're mostly bombed out.

Plants: Weeds, trees, brambles climbing over homes; bushes growing on children's playgrounds.

Animals: Wildlife living where humans should.

General Details

Backstory: During the Battle of Agdam, Armenian forces violated the rules of war by taking hostages, using indiscriminate fire, and forcibly displacing civilians. As the city fell, almost its entire population fled. The Armed Forces of Armenia still use the city as a buffer zone, meaning that Agdam remains empty and decaying, and usually off-limits for sightseeing.

Genre or Type of Scene: Spy thriller, fight scene, war story, historical drama, dystopia, fantasy world or science fiction.

People details

People: Usually military, as the ghost town is not open to the public.

Family/non-family friendly: Both, but it's too sad and lonely to explain to the young ones what happened here.

Sensory Details

Sights: Bullet pierced walls, cracks from bombing, a desolate and abandoned scene.

Smells: The natural earthy smells of vegetation overruling the ruins, yet the imagined tang of blood and odour of gunpowder during the war still hangs in the air.

Taste: Coppery taste of blood, biting gunshot dust on the back of the tongue, musky damp and decay.

Touch: The ruined walls feel rugged and rough, with thorns poking through the broken glass windows.

Sounds: Now silent and eerie, with the tweets of birds and barks of wild dogs, but during the war there was the terror of gunshots, bomb blasts and the rat-a-tat of constant firing.

Other Notes

You could use this as a dystopia setting and create a whole other world around the ruins. Or a historical story with another, similar, and war in mind. It looks like hell was unleashed in this place and even after the conflict was settled, nobody was interested in returning to this town. You can understand why. Who'd want to come back here in case the madmen returned?

Now Your Turn

Abandoned buildings are sad and lonely and conjure up images of all kinds of life that went on before the people left. Whole towns and villages are particularly wretched because floods of people would have had their lives destroyed. What is it about these places that make us want to set our stories here? The possibility of a life once lived, the imagined sounds of life bursting out of the buildings, and the vibrant colours of the cultures. All of this leads our imaginations to run riot and gather ideas for moving our characters in and out of these places.

If your character is working at theme parks that have been abandoned, he could travel to Spree Park in Berlin, Gulliver's Travel Park in Kawaguchi, Japan, Dadipark in Dadizel, Belgium, or Nara Dreamland in Japan, all of which will give your character lots of spooky experiences.

And don't forget to keep looking at my Pinterest board, which is crammed with more ideas: http://bit.ly/21JDdLg

Settings Can Make or Break a Scene

I love old abandoned buildings. There is something so beautiful, yet so sad about them, so I wanted to use one in my first novel, *The Grotto's Secret*.

I researched old mansions and found a few I liked, and used some elements of all three to make up my own fictional mansion. You can see mine here: http://bit.ly/1Zfn9Q4

My beta readers have said that the underground tunnel scenes in the book were electric, so much so that they couldn't put the book down. Not only did I use this setting for my climactic scenes, but I also used it for my fight scene. Additionally, going on Rayne Hall's advice from her book on fight scenes, I found lots of props and obstacles that both the villain and my heroine could use against each other.

Sliding Down the Cliffs

Name: Hallsands

Geographical Area: Devon, UK

Brief Description: Many of the UK's coasts suffer natural challenges from wind, rain, and wave-battered beaches and cliffs. Like a few others, the elements proved the undoing of this village, where beach erosion and the occasional fierce storm took their toll. In 1900, part of the village's sea wall was washed away, and by 1917 repeated strong gales and unusually high tides had made the village almost uninhabitable. A quick search will give you lots more examples where people's lives have been devastated by their homes falling into the sea.

USP: I love Torquay, where my husband and I used to spend a lot of time in our friend's holiday home. We trekked across the cliffs to a snug pub and on each visit we'd notice the slow decline of a house on the opposite bank. Maybe your character fought to have their cliffs stablised, only to end up watching their home slowly slide down the cliffs.

From Diamonds to Dust

Name: Kolmanskop

Geographical Area: Namibia.

Brief Description: Like many locations on the Southwest African coast, which is rich in diamonds, coal and gemstones, Kolmanskop became a thriving mining village in 1908. The mining community built houses and other amenities, including a hospital, ballroom, skittle alley, casino, and ice factory, in the architectural style of a German town. Only a few miles from the port of Lüderitz, Africa's first tram and the southern hemisphere's first X-ray station were also built here. When its diamond fields became depleted after the First World War, the town slowly died and was finally abandoned in 1954.

USP: This is a great setting for a historical romp of the Wilbur Smith ilk. Or your action hero could come steaming through here on his adventure through Africa. Even a thriller would be great here because maybe there are still diamonds in this mine and your character somehow finds out, only to have the big conglomerate corporations breathing down his neck.

Mother Nature Has Her Way

Name: Craco

Geographical Area: Gulf of Taranto, Italy

Brief Description: As a typical medieval hill town in the 'boot' of Italy built on a very steep defensive summit (400 metres) overlooking the Cavone River valley, Craco has a sad history.

In 1963, Craco had to be evacuated due to a landslide, triggered by infrastructure, sewer and water systems work being done in the town.

Then, in 1972, a flood caused further land slippage and worsened the situation further, preventing a possible repopulation of the historic town. Finally, in 1980, an earthquake showed that Mother Nature was determined to keep Craco free of people, and the city was completely and officially abandoned. Although Mother Nature believes she won her battle, the town fought back and is now a tourist attraction and a popular filming location.

USP: This wonderful setting with its old-world style is ideal for many genres, possibly every one of them if you wish to make up a new name for it and show it being lived in. Or let your story people do what they need to do to make it a real-life place. Or how about placing your character in the town as a resident and write about their experiences in a forces-of-nature thriller? Whatever you decide to do, this old city is crying out for some love. If you use it as a setting you will pay homage to its sad history.

Nuclear Disaster

Name: Pripyat City

Geographical Area: Ukraine

Brief Description: This once-busy city housed families of thousands of men and women who worked at the nearby Chernobyl Nuclear Power Plant.

But disaster struck this community when an explosion caused radiation to leak from its nuclear reactor on 26 April 1986. The entire city was evacuated and subsequently abandoned after the incident. And, regrettably, it will remain deserted for many thousands of years into the future.

USP: The city now resembles an apocalyptic setting, so you could set your story here and make up your own name for the location. Or your character could be investigating scientific disasters and come across this desolate place. What happens to your character? Will he find more leaks spreading into the water system, threatening the entire country? Or will two characters fall in love amidst the horrors of time gone by?

Fishing Island

Name: Baia dos Tigres

Geographical Area: Angola

Brief Description: Once a bustling fishing community in the Portuguese colonial era, this island was abandoned in 1974 because of strong winds, lack of drinking water and the transportation difficulties to the mainland, which was connected by a small sand causeway.

USP: If you're planning to have your international espionage thriller take place in many countries, this fishing village is one place your spy could stumble upon in their search for the truth behind the lack of fish in the sea.

What Can You Add to These 6 Sad Backdrops?

Any number of places in the world could be abandoned, so this one is easy enough to search and find. Just try Googling your genre

+ your story keywords + abandoned. See what you get, and let your imagination go.

More Setting Ideas

Put your character into one of these abandoned places: mansion, village, US western town, hospital, warehouse, factory, nursery, theme park, or nuclear facility.

Adventurous

These could be treacherous locations where adventurous heroes climb sheer cliffs or villains chase heroes through rainforests.

Wild Rain

Name: Madagascar Rainforest

Geographical Area: Madagascar

Brief Description: The eco-region constitutes a narrow strip of lowland forests between Madagascar's east coast and the mountainous central highlands, from sea level to 800 metres in elevation. It covers an area of approximately 112,600 square kilometres. The eco-region is under the direct influence of the moist southeast trade winds, which maintain a warm, humid climate.

USP: Madagascar is the fourth largest island in the world, and provides homes to a plant and animal mix, with the forests of the eastern plain being a particularly important aspect of this location. While it might conjure up images of a bunch of zoo characters stranded on the island, you could also raise the stakes by writing genres where ships could be hijacked by terrorists or political terror planes land on remote corners of the island. Maybe the President of the United States is being held captive here while unbeknownst to him, his family are cavorting with the British Prime Minister on the opposite end of this small stretch of land.

Mood Details

Mood: Tropical and dense, scary where the mangrove roots seem to want to reach out and grab you.

Colours: The scene is predominantly green laced with azure skies and ice blue sea.

Weather: Humid, warm, tropical, sticky and damp.

Visual: Tranquil golden beaches bordered by a safari land of wild animals cavorting through the canopy of trees of steaming rainforests.

Item Details

Ground: Rich, fertile soil, long sandy beaches, lush grasslands, boggy swamps, and rocky waterfalls.

Ceiling: Dense treetops prevent the sun from touching the ground of the rainforest.

Walls: The resorts have wooden walls, and some feature fabric tents for housing.

Doors: No doors are present in the wilderness, but in some places you'd think the rainforest had giant green doors (a metaphor, by the way) of ferns preventing visitors from coming to enjoy or destroy its secrets.

Props: Tree branches and leaves can be used to build rudimentary objects such as a hut or hunting instruments for your adventure-seeking hero.

Obstacles: Undergrowth of trees, no cellular or mobile reception, creatures that crawl out at night and bite or sting, and constant damp can hinder your character's pursuit or speed up the villain's escape.

Plants: The lowland forests have a rich diversity of Pandanus, bamboo, and orchid species.

Animals: Along with 41 mammals and 61 reptiles, Madagascar has several critically threatened species, including the Silky Sifaka, a lemur, which is one of the rarest mammals on earth. Your character will also find brown-tailed mongoose, reptiles, chameleons and freshwater fish.

General Details

Backstory: Sadly, there has been widespread slash-and-burn in the lowland rainforests, reducing forest habitats and adding survival pressures to some endangered species. Slash-and-burn is when locals cut and burn plants and forests to create fields for farming.

Genre or Type of Scene: Thriller, horror, survival adventure, political thriller, mystery, action adventure, fantasy.

People details

People: Local people enjoy working in tourism or agriculture.

Family/non-family friendly: Generally, family friendly; that's if your heroine isn't fazed by the widespread creepy-crawlies populating the forest undergrowth.

Sensory Details

Sights: Tall trees host a great variety of wildlife and protect the ground from the sun. Cool water ponds provide watering holes for the grassland animals.

Smells: If your characters are city slickers, the fresh air will invade their lungs as they smell the green grass obscured only by an earthy animal odour.

Taste: Depending which waterhole they drink from, the water could be brackish and rancid from animal droppings or a sweet, clear taste from a waterfall.

Touch: You can feel the soft touch of the forest's leaves as you run through this place, or feel the ripples of water cascading down the slippery rocks.

Sounds: Birds chirping and animals braying in a symphony of jungle song.

Other Notes

The baobab tree is also famous in this region. Maybe your fantasy characters live in one of these enormous trees. On holiday once in Rhodesia, my family and I all held hands with arms outstretched and formed a human chain to wrap ourselves around the tree. I seem to remember there were about ten to fifteen of us!

Now Your Turn

It's fun to search for and find adventure settings; the world literally is your oyster of amazing locations. Here's a few to whet your appetite:

Danger Highway

Name: Yungas Road

Geographical Area: Bolivia

Brief Description: As one of the most dangerous roads, therefore also known as Death Road, Yungas Road at San Pedro waterfall connects La Paz to Chulumani, 64 kilometres east of La Paz. Several years ago it was estimated that about 300 travellers were killed yearly along the road.

USP: The Yungas Road descends into the rainforest and winds through very steep hillsides and atop cliffs from northern Bolivia to the capital city. Your hero could be an action adventurer or a thrill-seeker on a terror quest. Either way, he'd better watch out, as the single-lane road twists and turns beside cliffs of up to 600 metres, with no guard rails. If he's travelling in the rainy season (November to March), rain and fog will severely hamper his visibility, and water runoff will turn the road in front of his jeep into a muddy track. Maybe he has to ditch his jeep and steal a mountain bike to join a group of bikers on the dangerous road when the road begins to crumble under his wheels. Will he survive the danger chasing him on the most dangerous road in the world?

Monk's Cave

Name: Phugtal Monastery

Geographical Area: Srinagar

Brief Description: Buddhist monks and nuns practice their religion in beautiful hills and high mountains where historical monasteries are known as Gompas. One such monastery is situated on the Wakha river valley between Kargil and Mulbekh, about 240 kilometres from Srinagar, and is a tough ascent halfway up a mountain slope.

It takes a tough, arduous trek of two or three days to reach this isolated monastery, which appears to be miraculously glued onto the side of a vertical rock-face. Known as one of the most secluded monasteries in the Zanskar region, the monastery lies at the opening of a giant cave. The cave is deserted on the front of a huge gorge that is also a passageway for a main tributary of the southern Lungnak River.

USP: If your character is after an adventurous experience, he can reach the monastery by trekking for a few days. When he reaches the honeycomb-like Phugtal Monastery, home to more than 70 monks, will the rest of the group still be alive? What or who has killed them off? Does your hero turn out to be the villain after some precious Buddhist relic, sculptures, murals or scripture that only the monks can reveal?

Beach Graveyard

Name: Skeleton Coast

Geographical Area: Namibia

Brief Description: Bleak, yet beautiful, Namibia's Skeleton Coast is one of the most primeval in the world.

The shores run from just north of the city of Swakopmund (a German settlement town) to the Angolan border in northwest

Namibia, raking in 500 kilometres of shoreline and 2 million hectares of dunes and gravel plains. This graveyard is strewn with rusting ship hulls from the many nautical victims, many from the former whaling industry, which gives the formidable coast this frightening name. Joining the remains of ships wrecked on the hidden rocks are fragments of bleached human and animal bones, such as seal skulls tossed about with turtle rib cages and the colossal, blanched vertebrae of whales. Portuguese sailors called it the Gates of Hell, while Namibia's Bushmen speak of the land God made in anger.

USP: The deep green sea, speckled with frothy surf that breaks over a shore and disappearing into infinite dunes, may fool your group of characters from the air. But after landing on the remote beach where the Benguela Current is forced inland by raging winds, the chill of the Atlantic won't cool them in the fierce heat of the Namib. Your group of airplane visitors definitely won't last long in this harsh environment. They will be restricted and need a permit. Or will they crash their private plane before they start their month's adventure to find that elusive wild elephant, the Mammoth, that is supposed to be extinct, now hairless and living in Africa?

4 Easy Escapades – Don't Stop There!

Depending on what action adventure your hero is taking, you could try searching for something like 'best river trips,' 'travel adventures,' 'daring escapes' or simply 'top 10 adventure holidays.' Or if your character is a female you could try 'best girlie adventures,' or possibly even 'kids' adventures.'

More Setting Ideas

Adventures can take place anywhere. How about a cliff's edge, on top of a mountain, on the edge of a balcony or roof, in or out of a moving vehicle, along a fast moving river, through a jungle, or in a city factory with dangerous equipment?

Country Life

Here we'll want peaceful meadows with lambs or wild and rugged wheat fields that families can enjoy—or where murders can take place.

Sand Spur

Name: Sable Island

Geographical Area: Canada

Brief Description: While Sable Island is a National Park Reserve, it's actually a tiny country island, which houses only five people. That number swells with tourists and scientists who arrive in the summer. Because it protects the unique Sable Island horse, the island is managed by Parks Canada.

USP: An estimated three hundred and fifty vessels are believed to have fallen victim to the island's sand bars. Maybe your story is looking for a setting that becomes the villain. This island could lure fishermen or luxury yachts to its shores, and who knows what goes on when they've been snared? Or you may want a pretty isolated place to unfold your love story, and this could be the perfect paradise.

Mood Details

Mood: Peaceful and calm, undisturbed by mankind.

Colours: The green meadows, deep blue sea, and golden sand dunes make up the perfect landscape in this island. Horses of different colours, mostly brown, catch your eye.

Weather: Sable Island's climate can be classified as either oceanic or humid continental. Its weather is strongly influenced by the sea.

Visual: Horses roaming freely in the meadow, from afar all you can see is a thin stretch of sand.

Item Details

Ground: Soil and asphalt. Sand and sea. Meadows and fields.

Ceiling: The sky is the ceiling in this beautiful, breath-taking decor.

Walls: White walls of the island station come into contrast with the black rooftops.

Doors: The Sable Island Station, managed and staffed by Parks Canada and Environment Canada, is the only permanently staffed facility on the island.

Props: Natural plants and stones, amongst manmade equipment available at the island station. Boats and nautical beach gear.

Obstacles: Thick fog, treacherous currents, and the island's location in the middle of a major transatlantic shipping route and rich fishing grounds account for the large number of wrecks.

Plants: It lacks native trees, being covered instead with marram grass and other low-growing vegetation.

Animals: The island is home to over four hundred free-roaming horses. Grey seals breed on the island's shores. Several large bird colonies are resident, including the Arctic tern and Ipswich sparrow, which only breeds on the island and is a subspecies of the Savannah sparrow.

General Details

Backstory: A life-saving station was established on Sable Island by the Governor of Nova Scotia, John Wentworth, in 1801. The Canadian government took over administration of the station and added two lighthouses in 1872, Sable Island East End Light on the eastern tip and Sable Island West End Light on the western end.

Genre or Type of Scene: This island is great for a ship wreck, either historical or modern.

People details

People: Permanent residents work at the island station, but your character will also meet temporary residents, such as scientists studying the flora and fauna.

Family/non-family friendly: Both, just don't let the kids get caught by the tides when they come in.

Sensory Details

Sights: The sand dunes and green meadows offer a magnificent impression of paradise.

Smells: Strong odour of salt in the air, earthy smell of the horses in the fields, sun lotion when tourists arrive. Acidic whiff of bird droppings drying on the rocks.

Taste: The sea air tastes salty. Sea water is bitter, gritty and sandy, with a fishy taste of kelp.

Touch: The meadow grass is spikey and spongey underfoot. Sea air salty and grainy on your skin. Sand is boggy and sucks at your feet when you run along the beach.

Sounds: Horses neighing. Bells in the tower. Ships' fog horns. Waves washing up the beach at high tide. Wind whistling along the shore. playing catch with sea shells.

Other Notes

What if murders are taking place, and a detective arrives to solve the crimes? Maybe a thriller where young lovers arrive on their yacht, only to find strange things going on. Could there be supernatural or science fiction oddities happening? Lots of genre possibilities. Maybe this remote island reminds your character of the freedom children feel when they are not yet grounded by society's rules.

Now Your Turn

Although Sable Island could be deemed as a seascape rather than a country life setting, you can pick and choose or combine as you plan your plot strands. It would be great for a children's or young adult adventure or fantasy.

Kaleidoscope Sand Dunes

Name: Chamarel Falls and the Colored Earth

Geographical Area: Mauritius

Brief Description: The beautiful island of Mauritius, formed by a now-dormant undersea volcano, is home to two natural wonders.

The tallest waterfalls on the island are the Chamarel Falls, which are three thin waterfalls that fall about 300 feet down a plateau. The island also has some amazing coloured dunes, which form when clay, made of lava, cools at different times. The multicoloured sand dunes that result from this process are stunning in shades of red, brown, violet, green, blue, purple, and yellow.

USP: The mystery to scientists trying to solve the strange properties of the sand is the fact that if you take all the colours and mix them together, they will naturally separate and re-join the correct colour grouping that they belong to. Another mystery they haven't solved is why there is no visible soil erosion. Could it be that your character is one of those scientists? And maybe they do indeed solve the mystery, which shocks the world.

Robben Hood

Name: Robben Island

Geographical Area: South Africa

Brief Description: Since the end of the 17th century, Robben Island has been used for the isolation of mainly political prisoners. Among its early permanent inhabitants were political leaders from various Dutch colonies.

In 1806 a Scottish whaler opened a whaling station at a sheltered bay on the north-eastern shore of the island, which became known as Murray's Bay. The island was also used as a leper colony and animal quarantine station.

Beginning in 1961, Robben Island was used as a prison for political prisoners and convicted criminals. It was also a maximum security prison for political prisoners until 1991. The medium security prison for criminal prisoners was closed in 1996, when Nelson Mandela was released.

USP: Was your character there to celebrate the famous release? Or was he a prison guard who spent his life in guilt? Whether they he friends or not with his famous prisoner, or even tried to help him escape, is up to you. Maybe you want a simple romance to brew between a prisoner and a guard? Either way, you have the makings of a story that is set on one of the most famous islands on earth.

Riot of Colour

Name: Caño Cristales

Geographical Area: Colombia

Brief Description: The world has some amazing places, as we've so far discovered, and Caño Cristales River, located in the Serrania de la Macarena Mountains, is another.

Normally, Caño Cristales is filled with waterfalls, rapids, wells and hollows, with water so clear you can see all the way to the bottom. But between September and November the clarity transforms, becoming a riot of colour. The algae in the water produces a colour-scape of red, blue, green, black and yellow, changing the river's name to 'The River of Five Colours.'

USP: So remote that your hero's family can only get there by horse, donkey, or on foot, this family adventure could turn into a blood river if your villain finds them. What do they have that he wants? And why?

Ruined Garden

Name: Lost Gardens of Heligan

Geographical Area: Cornwall, England

Brief Description: Twenty years ago entrepreneur Tim Smit battled through the blanket of brambles to discover Heligan's forgotten gardens. Today the magnificently restored Lost Gardens of Heligan boast more than two hundred acres of gardening marvels. For hundreds of years, Heligan's historic gardens were unknown and unseen because they were lost under a tangle of weeds. It was only the chance discovery of a door in the ruins that led to the restoration of this once-secret garden.

USP: Heligan, seat of the Tremayne family for more than four hundred years, is one of the most mysterious and romantic estates in England, with its secret garden lost for decades. Did your character grow up in the family? Maybe he discovered the garden or killed someone there and wanted the secret kept hidden. Whichever way you decide to go, and murders aside, this garden is magnificent, and a wonder for parents and kids alike. When you explore it for yourself, you'll find your imagination creeping into new lost corners of the gardens.

5 National Vistas, But Wait, There's More!

When you're next on holiday in the countryside, take note of all the things around you, from farm shops and barns to tractors and other farming kit.

But farming is not the only countryside pursuit; there could be country sports, country fairs, playgrounds, and woods and forests. Or search by country + genre+ story keywords.

More Setting Ideas

Will any of these settings work for you? Meadow, wheat field, maze, haystack, pond, farm, stables, woodland, village, barn, farmhouse, picnic area, lake side, village shop or bowling green.

Crowded Towns

Let's look at places with narrow streets and crowded markets and buildings with roof tops that beg for a chase scene.

Little Crowded Farm

Name: Rocinha

Geographical Area: Rio de Janeiro, Brazil

Brief Description: Compared to other favelas (little farms) across Brazil, in Rocinha you can find hundreds of businesses such as banks, medicine stores, bus lines and cable television. With a spectacular overview of Rio de Janeiro, Rocinha is believed to be home to more than seventy thousand people.

USP: Rocinha (little farm) is the largest favela in Brazil, and is located in Rio de Janeiro, built on a steep hillside overlooking the city. Many people could unknowingly watch a story taking place right on their doorstep.

Mood Details

Mood: Light, full of life

Colours: A rainbow of colours will be found in the favela, but rusty brick red, drab concrete grey and electric blue (water drums) stand out.

Weather: Hot and humid.

Visual: Most buildings have water tanks installed on the roof because water is a daily challenge; the water tanks are filled once a week.

Simile or Metaphor: This favela is as big as a small town and, due to the large number of inhabitants it hosts, it looks like it is about to explode at any minute.

Item Details

Ground: Most streets are made of asphalt, and the alleys are paved.

Ceiling: The building roofs are low and most have water tanks on them.

Walls: Most of the favela walls are made of brick or concrete, with a few painted in shades of avocado green and shades of yellow ranging from banana to lemon, but the majority remaining unpainted on the outside.

Doors: Many of the doors are made of metal and seem to lead into small, overpopulated apartments.

Props: You can find rental shops at every pace and drug dealers on every corner. To add to the hygiene problems, garbage litters the road, adding a spectral layer of stench to the tarmac.

Obstacles: To somebody new in the favela, the narrow alleyways will be obstacles for a character who is new to the favela especially if he's being chased or followed. Being able to find one's way in this overpopulated, agitated setting is a challenge.

Plants: Some trees are scattered across the favela, and the favela is almost entirely surrounded by a forest with olive-green bushes lining the steep banks behind the densely populated homes.

Animals: Stray dogs can be found lurking around almost every building, and your character will likely stumble over chickens strutting down the streets.

General Details

Backstory: The favela is located in Rio de Janeiro's South Zone between the districts of São Conrado and Gávea, with modular containers as housing.

Scene Type: A street chase in a fight scene would give your characters lots of problems.

Genre: Action, urban fiction, crime thriller, realistic fiction, drama or a tragedy, martial arts (lots of buildings to jump up and over), gangster, hardboiled or maybe a legal thriller where your hero decides to defend someone from this community and gets embroiled in their lives

People details

People: The people who live in the favela are generally poor, working class people who cannot afford better housing. Most of them are factory workers, trying to provide for their families. Those who are unemployed probably enjoy gossiping about the neighbourhood, and everybody seems to know everybody.

Family/non-family friendly: Families live in harmony here, but sure as hell will have gang warfare going on due to drug trade, so your characters wouldn't want to take their kids here on holiday.

Sensory Details

Sights: The favela is overpopulated, and the apartments appear to be small, compact or crowded with families living almost on top of each other.

Sun glares onto the mass of glass windows, sending flashes of bright light over the grim, discoloured buildings.

Smells: You can smell the typical Latin spices mixing up in dishes like Feijoada or Acaraje, garbage rotting on the street corners, sweaty bodies due to the water shortage, and, because some buildings appear to have outside toilets, there could be the occasional foul whiff of sewerage hanging in the air.

Taste: Chili is a fiery taste you can find in most dishes. Seafood, and in particular, fresh shrimp, is simmered in garlicky olive oil. Also to be found in home bakeries could be the Brazilian favourite — round morsels of hot cheesy bread, sweet pastries, croquettes and other salty pastries. Tapioca stands are common, as are those selling corn on the cob, coated in melted butter and sprinkled with salt. A popular beverage is coconut water, sucked from straws poking out of coconuts, tops hacked off expertly with machetes. The coconut is a perfect way to ward off dehydration, or to recover from the after-effects of a wild night out in this neighbourhood.

Touch: Hard concrete and hot pavement, greasy yet firm prawns, sticky tapioca, warm cheesy bread, wiry coconuts, sweaty bodies, hard plastic water tanks, soft and damp washing hanging off the lines, soggy plastic bags jamming the street corners.

Sounds: Scooters honk, seagulls squawk, gangsters yell, children cry, neighbours holler to each other over the roof tops, stall vendors shout to sell their wares, dogs bark and fight over the end of the day's pickings, chickens cluck along the streets, wild cats hiss at prowling dogs.

Other Notes

The açai berry is an Amazonian fruit ripe with antioxidants and anti-aging properties, and many credit it with promoting weight-loss. Its name comes from the Brazilian Portuguese adaptation of the Tupian word ïwaca'i,—fruit that cries or expels water. Maybe your character comes here to find out the secret to this amazing plant and gets caught up in this crowded culture.

Now Your Turn

With one full list above, go through the list below and create your own detailed setting from any of these places that inspire you. Remember to download my version so that you can work up your own scene settings. From the ideas below, add any other details you can think of, especially sensory details. Don't forget to add the personal and emotional details that only you will know about your character.

There are so many creative places where you could squash your hero into a crowded place and force her to get on with what she has to do to make your pages turn.

Subway Shove

Name: Subways in Tokyo

Geographical Area: Tokyo

Brief Description: Not only is Tokyo ridiculously crowded above ground, things don't change much down below.

It's home to the busiest subway system in the world, with millions passing through it every year. That's more than twice as many as New York City (although the NYC system has more stations). Another place is the Shibuya Crossing. With over two and a half million people crossing over the white stripes every day, Shibuya Crossing is said to be the busiest intersection in the world.

USP: If your action hero wants to lose himself, one of the best places to do that is ducking down into the Tokyo subways.

Shopping Spiral

Name: US Shopping Mall

Geographical Area: Minnesota

Brief Description: Although there are several shopping centres claiming to have the most traffic in the world (most being in Southeast Asia), my setting for the most crowded shopping plaza goes to the Mall of the America near the Twin Cities in Minnesota. It receives over 40 million annual visitors. That's some crowd!

USP: This is a fab place for your crime or thriller climax or fight scenes to take place. Thousands of people to crash into, lots of escalators shipping shoppers up and down, and a variety of expensive retail shops to in which to hide away.

Burning Your Bridges

Name: Busiest Bridge

Geographical Area: George Washington Bridge, USA

Brief Description: Carrying over 106 million cars across the Hudson River between New York and New Jersey every year, the George Washington Bridge is the world's busiest, so busy that it has two levels and a total of 14 lanes.

USP: Imagine your car chase landing up here and your villain gaining on your heroine, who only just learnt to drive a year ago and is one nervous-as-hell driver. How will she get across this bridge before the baddie and his gang gun her down? Jump? But she can't swim! Oh dear, there's no getting across here.

Shopping Heave-Ho

Name: Bright Lights of Oxford Street

Geographical Area: London

Brief Description: Oxford Street in London is lined with bars, hotels, and high-street shops and other expensive retailers. With all its attractions, over two hundred million people visit every year. Recently London authorities borrowed an idea from the Shibuya Crossing in Japan and reconstructed Oxford Circus and doubled the amount of pavement.

USP: A good obstacle for your protagonist is a dislocated shoulder. Just imagine the pain of being jostled about by all the pedestrians hustling to get into retail sales. I know all about this as I had to pass through Oxford Street (not to shop) with a dislocated shoulder. With each person pushing past me, I felt like my shoulder was coming undone again. Give your heroine an injury or ailment like this in a crowded town and you're sure to see her true colours coming through.

By the Thousands

Name: Mongkok District

Geographical Area: Hong Kong

Brief Description: The most crowded place in the world is the Mongkok commercial and residential district found in Hong Kong. With over 340,000 people per square mile, nothing else on Earth comes even close.

USP: Your crime thriller would take a sharp turn if the protagonist had to visit Hong Kong. She'd be scared of flying of course, because landing a plane between high-rise buildings and onto a short and narrow landing strip will set her nerves on edge. Never mind sending her down these streets to find a lead that will solve the crime.

People Carriage

Name: Crowded train in India

Geographical Area: India

Brief Description: Although Tokyo has its fair share of crowded areas, along with Hong Kong and New York and some parts of London, India's train system wins hands down when it comes to crowded trains. On the roof, hanging out the window, up the sides, under the carriage – you name a part of the train that someone can't sit on, and I'll tell you that you're lying. See my image on the Scene Settings Pinterest board to see how you cannot even see the train for the hordes of people.

USP: Your character will need to be for a long, long ride on this journey because often these trains just stop in the middle of nowhere for who-knows-what reason.

Maybe your character is the train driver and has to escape from one of his hundreds or thousands of passengers. He stops the train, abandons it and runs off where? And who follows him?

Russian Needle

Name: Kresty Prison

Geographical Area: St. Petersburg, Russia

Brief Description: The only downside (except for being starved and beaten) is that Kresty Prison in St. Petersburg was built to hold only 3,000 people, yet now it houses more than ten thousand prisoners. Almost a person for each square metre. If your characters landed up in here, they wouldn't want to be claustrophobic. Or would they?

USP: Going to prison in Russia is probably not on your list of to-dos for your heroine, but when she follows a lead in your conspiracy thriller or mystery, she could end up trying to find a Russian needle in this haystack of convicts.

Denser Than Dense

Name: Manila.

Geographical Area: Manila, Philippines.

Brief Description: If you thought New York City was crowded, think again. With only about 30,000 people per square mile, it's pretty much a desert compared to Manila. As the capital of the Philippines, and the most densely populated city in the world, Manila has over 110,000 people per square mile.

USP: Endless opportunities to get chased, hide, escape, get run down by drug dealers, get shot or stabbed ... the list goes on.

9 Neck of the Woods; Just the Beginning

City streets, sidewalks or pavements are usually crowded, along with bustling small towns. Churches or chapels can also be crowded, or they could be desolate if it's a weekday with no weddings or other events taking place. Universities are another ideal location with lots of people milling about, if your story requires bodies en-mass. Try famous ones such as Cambridge and Oxford in the UK or Harvard and UCLA in the USA, or go for a small, local uni that is just as hectic. Just search for the kind of crowded place that fits with your genre storyline.

More Setting Ideas

Try these for size: Market place, souk, rooftop, back yard, town library, busy factory, industrial estate, or narrow streets between houses.

Down Below

Let's delve underground into tunnels and caves.

Trenched In

Name: Củ Chi tunnels

Geographical Area: Vietnam

Brief Description: Originally the location of several military campaigns during the Vietnam War, and the Viet Cong's base of operations for the Tết Offensive in 1968, the Củ Chi tunnels are preserved in their original form and are now open to visitors.

USP: Because the tunnels were so important to the Viet Cong in their resistance to American land and air forces, and because food and water were so scarce, maybe your character is a spy who only wants out of this hell-hole, so he will offer his knowledge to the highest bidder. Would that be the US government? If he sneaks into the Viet Cong's operational base, will his comrades find out and give him up for food for their families?

Mood Details

Mood: Spooky and claustrophobic, musty and damp, with a sense that it's hard to breathe.

Colours: Different shades of browns and greys.

Weather: Hot on the outside, cool in the trenches.

Visual: Camouflaged trap doors used to access the tunnels.

Item Details

Ground: Brown mouldy stone underfoot; some paths leading up to the tunnel are jungle, full of decaying leaves and broken twigs.

Ceiling: Brown stone and concrete.

Walls: More brown stone with mould growing in damp areas.

Doors: Wooden, and usually camouflaged with leaves and bamboo sticks.

Props: Rocks, hidden doors, lots of old war artifacts.

Obstacles: You can easily get lost in the tunnels. If your hero's flashlight runs out of battery, he'll be in trouble.

Plants: Inside the tunnels, mould on the walls from humidity.

Animals: Ants, poisonous centipedes, scorpions, spiders and vermin all crawling in the dark, damp corners.

General Details

Backstory: The 75-mile tunnels were used by Viet Cong soldiers as hiding spots during combat, as well as serving as communication and supply routes, hospitals, food and weapon caches, and living quarters for numerous North Vietnamese fighters.

Genre or Type of Scene: Survival, spy thriller, political thriller, horror.

People details

People: Tourists are allowed in the open tunnels. Some people may enter the restricted areas of the tunnels.

Family/non-family friendly: Both if you're writing a kid's spy thriller.

Sensory Details

Sights: Above-ground attractions include caged monkeys, vendors selling souvenirs, and a shooting range where visitors can fire a number of assault rifles. Inside is dark and scary, tight and narrow with shadows creeping along the tunnels.

Smells: Damp and musty, suffocating with the rancid smell of urine and dead rats.

Taste: You can almost taste the sulphur from the gunpowder stored here from ages ago.

Touch: Cold stone, ragged crevices, slimy walls dripping with algae water.

Sounds: A constant drip over the entrance ceiling. The wind howls in the tunnels, slams a metal door, clangs and sends a rumble back up the tunnel to greet your characters. Will they go in after all that?

Other Notes

Claustrophobics should not enter these tunnels, unless your protagonist needs to endure a bit of torture. Which of course, your readers will love, so they can worry about him struggling to breathe as he escapes to get his spy info into the highest-bidding hands. It feels like there is no more air left, and that the walls of the tunnel are closing in on your character. Could he suffer from asthma?

Now Your Turn

Settings down below lend themselves seamlessly to a scary, spooky or chilling story, be that any kind of hair-raising genre. Any of the places below could be fictional, too, so don't restrict your imagination if something doesn't fit; use what you can and toss in your own flavours.

The Big Man-Made Hole

Name: The Big Hole, Open Mine, Kimberley

Geographical Area: South Africa

Brief Description: The Big Hole in Kimberley is claimed to be the largest hole excavated by hand. In 1871, with a diamond rush in the area, a group of workers were scratching around at the base of Colesberg koppie, a small hill on the De Beers brothers' farm. In its heyday, tens of thousands of miners swarmed over the land to work their ten-square-metre claim, and a network of ropes and pipes crisscrossed the surface. Eventually the hole was dug to a depth of 240m entirely by pick and shovel, and remains one of the largest manmade excavations in the world. By 1914, when De Beers closed the mine, some 22.6 million tons of earth had been removed, yielding over 13.6 million carats (2722kg) of diamonds.

USP: If you're writing a historical story of this big hole down under, you'll show how lives were lost and fortunes discovered and squandered.

You'll show how the mine became too dangerous from the top, and a shaft was dug to allow further excavations beneath it to a depth of over 800m. Maybe your character is the first person to find a diamond, yet remained poor until his death. Or one of the De Beer Brothers who raked in a fortune?

Cave Delight

Name: Neversink Preserve

Geographical Area: Jackson County, Alabama

Brief Description: This 162-foot open-air pit is loved by cave explorers, and when you see the images on my Pinterest board you'll see why. It's probably the most scenic pit that exists, with its beautiful fern-covered ledges of vegetation and waterfalls. Forty feet in diameter at the top, it bottoms out to one hundred feet in diameter.

USP: As the spring is the only reliable water supply for a home at the bottom of the mountain, could your character be in a tangle to buy the cave? Does he succeed? Or maybe he's a photographer on a world hunt for the best cave to win photography awards? Does someone get there first? Does he fall in love with her?

Below Decks

Name: Lotofaga

Geographical Area: Samoa, South Pacific

Brief Description: In the To Sua Ocean Trench, the island of Upolu was formed by a massive basaltic shield volcano. With it came this incredible natural swimming hole, which is only accessible via a long ladder and small dock.

USP: Does your character come out from nearby New Zealand to swim in the hole, only to find a strange underwater creature never seen before?

What Creeps Beneath

Name: Underground Stations

Geographical Area: London

Brief Description: There's something eerie yet compelling about lost underground stations. That's probably why many classics feature them as a setting. From classic *Doctor Who*, to *An American Werewolf in London*, and *Sherlock*. As the world's first underground rail network, the London Underground is manic most days, but this one will no doubt be silent, hidden and deeply spooky, with shadows lurking behind steel doors.

USP: Thrilled by the peculiar creepiness of an empty platform, or simply looking for a silent ghost station, your character could end up in a subterranean drama taking place so far below ground that no one knows he's there.

5 Downcasts Here; Now, What Else?

Stations like Kings Cross, Waterloo, or any of the busy US stations would be easy to research. But what about war tunnels, caves, sink holes, and even graveyards?

More Setting Ideas

Have your character in these places: water reservoir tunnel, cave, cellar, basement, jail, cavern, vault, sewer, grave, or labyrinth.

Historical

A must for writing historical fiction is finding old places in history. This topic is an exciting one for me, as I am writing a medieval conspiracy thriller, which zips back and forth between medieval Spain and modern-day London

The day my husband and I stepped onto a property which would eventually become our new home in Spain, I was inspired by the view down the Guadalhorce Valley between Malaga and Marbella and beyond. Apart from a white-washed village in the distance, all we could see were layers upon layers of shadowy mountains. In that instant a medieval character popped into my head and I imagined her right there in that valley. It became the fictional setting for *The Grotto's Secret*.

So, if you're writing historical fiction, I hope one of these old places inspires you to write a fabulous novel.

Watch for what Glenn Cooper has to say about hooking your reader into your historical setting in the last chapter on 'location.'

Kings Wadi

Name: The Valley of the Kings

Geographical Area: Egypt

Brief Description: The valley stands on the west bank of the Nile, within the heart of the Theban Necropolis.

The 'Wadi' of the Kings has two valleys, East Valley (where most of the royal tombs are found) and West Valley. For a period of nearly

500 years, from the 16th to 11th century BC, tombs were constructed for the Pharaohs and powerful nobles of the New Kingdom (the Eighteenth to the Twentieth Dynasties of Ancient Egypt).

USP: A Wadi is the old Arabic reference to a valley, which sometimes meant a dry riverbed. This location would be ideal for many genres. Because of its very nature, lots of historical conspiracy thrillers have used places in Egypt, but it could be just as good for an action adventure, horror scene or crime thriller because of the many threats a hero could face. Equally, your travel-weary heroine could fall in love with an Egyptian guide in your romance.

Mood Details

Mood: Frightening, spooky, awe-inspiring.

Colours: The predominant colour in this setting is golden sand, combined with shafts of ivory-white stone pyramids.

Weather: Dry and hot with occasional sand storms, which could be a great obstacle to scupper your protagonist.

Visual: Miles and miles of sand with wonderfully designed pyramids rising up to meet cloudless skies, with the tomb entrances embedded into the natural landscape.

Simile or Metaphor: It feels like the spirits of past rulers of Egypt still watch over the country. They seem to loom over anyone who passes by their sacred resting place.

Item Details

Ground: The ground is covered in shingle and, during sand storms, the public alleys get covered in silt. The types of soil in the valley are an alternating sandwich of dense limestone and other sedimentary rock, and soft layers of marl.

Ceiling: While the tombs have been carved in the natural layout of the valley, the ceilings of the burial chambers were lovingly decorated.

Walls: Dense limestone or sedimentary rocks make up the walls of the tombs, which are painted and decorated with religious texts and images. The early tombs were decorated with the journey of the sun god through the twelve hours of night to ensure the tomb owner's safe passage through the night.

Doors: Usually the tomb plan involved a long rock-cut corridor, descending through one or more halls so the entrances were often hidden and thus hard to find.

Props: An assortment of items in the tombs, assuming they weren't ransacked. Each tomb owner was buried with equipment that would enable a continued and comfortable existence in the afterlife, so many of these items can be used as props, depending on which tomb your story follows. Ritual magical items, such as Shabtis and divine figurines were also buried in the tombs and would be good to add another dimension to your plot.

Obstacles: Many of the tombs are unstable, and during an earthquake could collapse. In addition, many others have been ransacked and many walls broken down, giving your villain lots of places to hide or trap your hero.

Plants: The Valley of Kings is a desert wadi devoid of natural vegetation. But you could imagine new plant life if you were using this as a setting for a magical tale or fantasy.

Animals: Mice are lured by the leftovers of tourists so be sure your heroine is terrified of rats and rodents. Characters may also encounter snakes, scorpions, insects, small birds and bats in certain tombs. In your fantasy, you could make up some horrific-looking creatures who live on the remains of the Kings. Or your science fiction novel could see aliens landing here to take back their 'people' and stop the marauding tourists. How they do that is up to you.

General Details

Backstory: The valley is known to contain sixty-three tombs and chambers, ranging in size from a simple pit, to complex tombs with hundreds of chambers.

Genre or Type of Scene: Journey or travel saga, fight scenes, conspiracy theory, thriller, horror, action adventure, political or spy thriller or historical novel.

People details

People: Lots of colourful people, from locals and tourists to tourism staff and archaeologists. Or the aliens who land to take back their pyramids. And of course, the people of the new fantasy world you create.

Family/non-family friendly: Both, depending on your storyline.

Sensory Details

Sights: Sand, secret corridors, hidden entrances, religious decorations in the tombs.

Miles of valleys, a gleaming river winds like a snake between the tombs, golden sunsets shooting shards of amber over the pyramids.

Smells: Musky, tangy odours from tombs infested with fungi and bacteria; the stench of ammonia and urine from tourists who have desecrated the sacred burial grounds; damp, musty with no fresh air to drive off the old decaying fumes.

Taste: Salty, sweaty and often dry mouth due to the heat. Your character may love the rich spicy Egyptian food yet despise the sour bitterness of the local brews.

Touch: When you touch the walls of the burial sites, you feel little particles of sand sticking to your sweaty fingers. Gritty and dry and hard to the touch. Cold air on your skin when your hero crawls into this uninviting place. An eerie feeling hangs thick in the air, almost reaching down and touching them like a spider's web.

Sounds: Peaceful and quiet-, but sometimes you can hear the sound of mice or bats in the tombs. Or the hissing of the sand as it stings your hero's face in a sand storm, and the wind whistling down the secret tomb corridors. If you have a ghost story in mind, maybe your hero hears the tomb's King or noble waking from the dead at a certain hour and marching up and down, ordering his men to seal up the tomb.

Other Notes

The royal tombs were decorated with scenes from Egyptian mythology and give clues to the beliefs and death rituals of the period. Depending on your story, you could research the different tomb decorations, and their mythology or rituals will add lots of plot threads.

New discoveries in 2005 and 2008 prove that there are undiscovered tombs still to be found, so when your hero discovers a new tomb with the help of his Egyptian girlfriend and her brother, it could be another principal burial place of a major royal figure of the Egyptian New Kingdom, or one of the privileged nobles.

Now Your Turn

History is rich with ideas and location settings. From the troubles of Scotland to the fiery French Revolution and the savages of the Spanish Inquisition, history has so many mysteries that are yet to be written.

And there is also the possibility of writing a historical saga or romance. Why not consider a historical fantasy or combine the seascapes with some history settings so you have a historical/nautical story?

Ancient Temple

Name: Ta Prohm temple

Geographical Area: Cambodia

Brief Description: The Cambodian temple of Ta Prohm shows just how ancient it is with an old tree growing through the ruins over the passage of time. Originally built in the twelfth century as Rajavihara, Ta Prohm, it was home to eighteen high priests, but was abandoned nearly four hundred years ago.

USP: As it's a popular place to visit, your romance story could start or end here if your characters are travelling or looking for religion and peace. But then, what if this temple held secrets that could affect the modern world? A great setting for a thriller or mystery too.

Ceremonial Jars

Name: Plain of Jars

Geographical Area: Xieng Khouang Province, Laos

Brief Description: Shrouded in myth, megalithic stone jars are scattered across Xieng Khouang Province in groups from one to one hundred. One theory is that the huge cylindrical jars were used in ancient funeral ceremonies. Other local legends suggest that the jars were used to brew rice wine for giants.

USP: In the 1960s, Northern Laos was subject to a massive aerial bombardment by the USA, so it could be a historical setting for a war novel or even modern day story that slips back in time, to show how and why and what your fictional people really did with these jars.

Original Conspiracy Theory

Name: Nazca Lines

Geographical Area: Pampa de San José, Peru

Brief Description: Animal figures and geometric shapes etched by the ancient Nazca into Peru's barren Pampa de San José can only be viewed in its entirety from the air. This is one of South America's great mysteries so a historical storyline with the Nazca culture would fit snugly between the lines.

USP: The Nazca lines are the original conspiracy theory. Stories fly around about who actually created these perfect drawings that can only be appreciated from the sky. Does your hero find out that this is evidence of a higher culture from an extra-terrestrial visit? Maybe your hero was flying over, became distracted and crashed into the midst of the lines. What happens next?

Resisting The Fight

Name: Secret Bunker

Geographical Area: Selkirk, Scottish Borders

Brief Description: Seventy years after World War Two a secret bunker was found and said to be used by civilian spies and saboteurs trained in guerrilla warfare.

USP: With a main chamber and a series of escape tunnels that would have been guarded by resistance soldiers, this could be used in a dystopia setting for when your world has ended with only a few people remaining to build a new one. It could be used for a zombie or horror novel. Maybe your character was the one who found this bunker when a group of friends shimmied down a shaft into inky blackness, only to find rusted weapons such as .38-calibre pistols, Sten guns, Thompson submachineguns, Tommy guns, commando knives and plastic explosives, along with food tins. Amongst all of this, their shocking find is lost world war secrets.

Museum Painting Studio

Name: Islamic Museum

Geographical Area: High Street, Kensington, London

Brief Description: Extraordinary Arab hall, now a Museum, with golden dome, intricate mosaics and walls lined with beautiful Islamic tiles. Upstairs has a vast painting studio filled with paintings in different stages of completion and lit by a great north window.

USP: If you have a political thriller on your hands, this stunning building could be a fun place for your heroine to get lost or chased into, or even closeted inside for some reason. Possibly something to do with the painting studio. Maybe the villain is forging or stealing famous art with this setting as his lair.

6 Yester Years Are Only a Taste

Just because you're told to 'write about what you know' doesn't mean you have to limit yourself. I've always loved writing about historical events, and when I first started writing I was very disappointed when an agent told me 'history is dead.' Thank goodness several famous historical authors have injected new life into the historical genre.

World wars, medieval England, Spain or France, Regency England, the Wild West, and country battles will give you ideal settings. There have been so many historical happenings, people and places that will inspire characters and settings. From castles and caverns to ships and subs, history is a wonderfully rich place for stories to take place, all giving your reader a whole new world to experience. And a new slice of history to grab their interest.

I didn't know much about medieval Spain until I stepped onto the property which would become my new home in Spain, only to have a feisty young medieval lady pop into my head. I imagined her and other fictional people out there in the hills and valley. I was so intrigued by her that I followed her lead and learnt as much as I could about her world. That's the exciting part about being a writer!

More Setting Ideas

A few tried and tested ideas come to mind: castle, palace, ballroom, workhouse, cathedral, ruin, or below stairs in a posh mansion.

Modern Techno

Space age buildings or futuristic designs.

Worlds Colliding

Name: Water Discus Hotels

Geographical Area: Dubai

Brief Description: As there are lots of wonderful places privately or commercially owned, I have specifically not shown any commercial locations because that's not the kind of book I wanted to create. However, in this particular section it was a bit more difficult to decide whether to include one or not. I chose to do so simply because this one is so unusual, and it is a prime example of modern technology in architecture. The spectacular building of the Water Discus Hotels comprises two discs: an underwater and above-water disc.

USP: Although the structure has been built to the highest safety standards that will withstand any weather, even a tsunami, maybe you want to use this setting for your fictional Mother Nature thriller. Or possibly a setting for a science fiction story or a fantasy world.

Mood Details

Mood: Romantic and light

Colours: The underwater scene is multicoloured, with the blue sea standing out. The fish are of vivid nuances of orange, green, blue and red.

Weather: Hot and sunny.

Visual: The helipad can be the perfect place for an action or fight scene.

Simile or Metaphor: The two main hotel reception discs look like UFOs.

Item Details

Ground: The hotel has concrete on the outside, square tiles in the inside common parts and wood flooring in the apartments.

Ceiling: The flat ceiling has an imprint of the reflection of light in the water outside the hotel.

Walls: The walls are simple and made of concrete and glass. Apartments in the underwater disc have a large glass window, so that guests may observe the marine life.

Doors: Wooden doors are present in the apartments.

Props: Typical of hotel rooms, which include: chairs, towels, bedding, but you also have the beach and surrounding, so you can include small boats like a rubber dinghy if your character is being chased.

Obstacles: Waiters, other tourists, and many hotel or beach props.

Plants: Algae, other water plants and brilliant sea life.

Animals: Multicoloured fish; or maybe your hero is sent to discover the underwater sea monsters slowly killing guests.

General Details

Backstory: This combination of underwater and above-water views will allow guests to admire the depths of the ocean while making the most of the warm climate.

The two parts of the structure are connected by three solid legs and a vertical shaft containing a lift and stairway.

Genre or Type of Scene: Romantic, comedy, thriller, fantasy, science fiction.

People details

People: Wealthy tourists; only the crème de la crème can afford this kind of destination.

Family/non-family friendly: Family friendly, maybe your characters are spoilt brats travelling the world for the best destinations.

Sensory Details

Sights: The two brightly lit discs look like UFOs floating on the sea, their glittering lights shimmering down into the shadowy depths.

Smells: The smell of sea water and sand with the random whiff of tropical sun lotion from terrace sunbathers. Rich mouth-watering smells rise from the outdoor dining areas.

Taste: Platters of fresh seafood will be succulent and spicy accompanied by full-bodied wine or zesty freshly squeezed fruit juice.

Touch: Your diving character gets slippery wet from the great expanse of water surrounding the hotel, as he dives amongst the many beautiful sea creatures, most of them cold and scaly with the occasional rubbery skin on a tame dolphin.

Sounds: The sound of freshly caught fish flapping, tourists chatting amongst themselves while they sunbathe, glasses chinking when iced drinks are poured, lobsters sizzling on the barbeque grill.

Now Your Turn

Get out your pen and start scribbling notes to get you in the mood to come up with the most outrageous techno setting. Anything from a tall, magnificent shape to a modern gargoyle lump.

Towering View

Name: Faro de Moncloa

Geographical Area: Madrid

Brief Description: In 1990, Salvador Pérez Arroyo was commissioned to design the structure in preparation for Madrid being the European Capital of Culture in 1992. This futuristic tower stands 110 metres high with an observation deck with 400 square metres of surface area, accessible by a lift inside the main shaft and boasting a view of northwest Madrid and the surrounding Guadarrama mountains.

USP: Maybe your character is a tree-hugging Spaniard who fought the building of this mod-monstrosity with its 1,200 cubic metres of concrete, and 10,000 tons of steel. His group felt that it broke the natural aesthetics of the area, looking too metallic and futuristic amid the more conservative buildings. Maybe he met and fell in love with another environmentalist. Or better still, an architect on the project so there was immediate conflict between them before they finally found a way to compromise.

Outer Space

Name: International Space Station

Geographical Area: Space

Brief Description: This one is only up your street if you're writing science fiction or a drama about space travel. This International Space Station is one of the most remote places in the universe.

USP: With its permanent crew of six people inhabiting a total livable area of about 43,000 cubic feet (the size of about three houses), your character would need to have a pretty damn good reason to land up in here. But then again, maybe you use this as inspiration for your own space station and give your characters' lots of reasons to fight each other in this claustrophobic space.

Twin Towers Barefoot Climb

Name: Petronas Twin Towers, Kuala Lumpur City

Geographical Area: Malaysia

Brief Description: A pair of buildings in the Kuala Lumpur City Centre rise 1,483 feet (452 m) into the air, and are the tallest twin towers in the world. Along with nearby Kuala Lumpur Tower, the buildings are a prominent landmark of Kuala Lumpur.

USP: Events that are attributed to this building include a record for base jumping and the evacuation of thousands of people in 2001 after a bomb threat was phoned in the day after the September 11 attacks destroyed the World Trade Center towers in New York City.

Thankfully, Bomb Disposal squads found no bomb in the Petronas towers. One of the most notable events was when a French urban climber used his bare hands and feet and no safety devices to scale to the top of Tower Two in just under two hours. Although arrested, he tried again a few years later. Could any of these events be the basis of your story? Or the inspiration to create a story with a similar setting?

Basket Case

Name: The Basket Building

Geographical Area: Ohio, United States

Brief Description: Despite it looking like a cute wicker picnic basket kept in the park, this seven story concrete building is an office.

USP: Due to its length, width, and breadth, and its wide roofline, this building would be a fabulous place to stage a whacky comedy or a strange warped thriller.

Otherworldly Space Cup

Name: The Niteroi Contemporary Art Museum

Geographical Area: Brazil

Brief Description: Another alien-looking building, this museum looks as though a flying saucer has just landed atop a cliff overlooking the ocean. The journey inside is said to be simply out of this world.

USP: If you're creating a science fiction series this setting supplies all sorts of possibilities. You could use the beach below to add conflict or ignore it altogether and place your setting somewhere else. Either way you'd have an original setting that looks very otherworldly.

Egg-stra Terrestrial

Name: National Centre for the Performing Arts

Geographical Area: China

Brief Description: This is space age deluxe. Although the National Centre for the Performing Arts took almost six years to be built, it showed architectural brilliance. It resembles an enormous lit-up egg lying in an artificial lake, but it's all made of titanium and glass.

USP: An alien storyline or science fiction novel would suit this setting down to the ground. Although, in saying that, many other genres would be just as suitable with a dusting of imagination. The mirror effect of the glistening lake gives it all sorts of possibilities where a writer could really take this modern techno setting to the extreme!

6 Tech-Moderns Barely Scratch the Surface

Now that you have 6 modern settings, why not go find more? There will be thousands more excellent places to research if you need something high-tech.

Google your genre + modern buildings or your genre + Space age buildings or futuristic designs. If none of these work for you, there will be lots out there to choose. Be creative when you search, for instance try something like 'the world's most space age designs.'

More Setting Ideas

Maybe you'd like to explore these ideas: Space Centre, eco building, space ships, futuristic transport, space station or a super geeky computer lab.

Mountains and Valleys

Exceptional mountains or winding valleys where the villain can chase the hero.

Steaming Hot

Name: Land of Fire and Ice

Geographical Area: Russia

Brief Description: The valley has the second largest concentration of natural geysers of hot springs in the world. About ninety of them are situated on the Kamchatka Peninsula in the Russian Far East, beside the deep waters of the Geysernaya River.

USP: Miles and miles of valleys and hills oozing steam and sulfuric acids could be what you plan for your unsuspecting characters out in Russia or your fantasy world setting. Caldrons of geothermal waters may flow into or out of this setting, and could set them back many times as you figure out your plot points.

Mood Details

Mood: Frightening because it looks like an uninhabited region covered in fog, with steam belching out of every mountain top.

Colours: Brown and green are predominant, and are combined with the silver-grey billows of steam.

Weather: Kamchatka's climate has cool winters and warm summers, with these geysers pulsing all year-round.

Visual: The waters in the valley are a beautiful turquoise, akin to a gemstone.

Simile or Metaphor: It looks like the place where dinosaurs once lived happily.

Item Details

Ground: Soil of different types with lots of sheer rock and shale mountains to climb.

Ceiling: The mountain tops are often covered in fog so you never see any sky. Unless you're a dragon who flies.

Walls: There are certain volcanoes in the area and caves with slimy walls— is that where dragons hang out? Or concoct magical spells?

Doors: The doors to your fantasy world could be a cavern hidden behind a rock face or a spring of hot water, where the dragon has to squeeze through to get the potion to continue living a normal dragon's life.

Props: Things to get in anyone's way (dragon or otherwise) can be found in nature, like rocks, sticks, herbs; never mind the hot, sweaty steam, which could be poisonous if you put your imagination to it.

Obstacles: The water, the geysers, volcanoes, steam jets.

Plants: Over 700 species of plants, but who is stopping you from creating more?

Animals: Brown bears and lots of salmon, if your dragon fancies sushi.

General Details

Backstory: Local scientist, Tatyana Ustinova, discovered rows and rows of pulsating hot spring geysers in 1941. She published her findings fourteen years later, but there was little exploration of the area until 1972.

Genre or Type of Scene: Action adventure, mystery, thriller, fantasy, crime, magic, horror, folklore, mythic, sword and sorcery, historical, science fiction.

People details

People: Tourists and scientists alike can only reach the valley by helicopter, so your hero has to be pretty rich to get here. Unless it's a fantasy or science fiction imaginary world.

Family/non-family friendly: Both, that's if the heroine's little kid or adopted niece is not scared of dragons.

Sensory Details

Sights: Beautiful geysers pulsate out of the ground amidst clouds of salty steam. The sun sparkles on the wide volcanic lakes.

Smells: Close to the geysers a damp, musty odour hangs in the air. Too close and the noxious stench could make your POVs eyes water.

Taste: If the hero is a magician, he could taste herbs used for medicine, or to get rid of the bitter, acidic taste of the Sulphur geyser in the air.

Touch: You know that feeling you get when getting close to a steaming kettle, sticky and sweaty? Well, don't let your hero put his hand over any one of these geyser kettles; it won't just singe his skin, it could take his arm off.

Sounds: Birds chirp, steam hisses, water gushes over rocks, stones crash to the craggy river and flop into the water.

Other Notes

Maybe your Jurassic story takes place here, or your fantasy world with dragons who thrive on the steam from the geysers. Maybe your hero is that very dragon who has to stop the villain dragon from corking up the steam springs and ending life on earth for all Russian dragons.

Now Your Turn

If you've been to a mountainous region you only need to imagine what it would be like filled with pot-holes of stinking steam. Get your list out to create your own file of settings. From the ideas below, add any other details you can think of, especially sensory specifics and your character's personal particulars and the emotions she will experience.

If your storyline could do with a valley or two, here are some exceptional valleys you may want to research: Semu Champay, Guatemala, Bohinj Valley, Slovenia, Hunaz Valley, Pakistan, Squaq Valley, California, Castle Valley, Utah, Manoa Valley, Hawaii, Grisedale Valley, UK and the Yosemite Valley, California.

Most mountain regions are perfect for romance or an action romp, but they'd be just as good for crime, political tales or even slipstream, supernatural fiction or a disaster thriller, especially where natural forces could play a big character role.

Globetrotting Mountaineer

Name: The Andes

Geographical Area: South America

Brief Description: The longest continental mountain range in the world is The Andes. Its continual stretch of highlands along the western coast is seven thousand kilometres wide and features peaks reaching up four thousand kilometres into the sky.

USP: If you want your characters to globetrot, placing them in The Andes will see them travelling north to south through seven South American countries: Venezuela, Colombia, Ecuador, Peru, Bolivia, Chile and Argentina.

Spanish Nevada

Name: Sierra Nevada

Geographical Area: Andalucía, Spain

Brief Description: The Sierra Nevada is a spectacular mountain range in the region of Andalucía, spanning across the provinces of Granada and Almeria in Spain. Meaning 'snowy range' in Spanish, it boasts the highest point of continental Spain, Mulhacen at 3,478 metres above sea level. Walking in the surrounding area is as scenic as in the Sierra itself. In the shadow of the Sierra Nevada lies the historic city of Granada, which, with its rich history, could make for a great start of a historical thriller or mystery.

USP: Your character will find lots of reasons to be here, from skiing the high peaks to sunning on the nearby Mediterranean Sea. She could get caught up in the plot of your story from Granada to Almeria and Malaga. Or further afield if need be.

American Nevada

Name: Sierra Nevada

Geographical Area: California

Brief Description: The Californian Sierra Nevada spans north to south for 400 miles. It has several notable features: Lake Tahoe with its large alpine lake, Mount Whitney's highest point, and the Yosemite Valley, which has been sculpted by glaciers out of 100-million-year-old granite.

USP: The Sierra is home to three national parks with many wilderness areas and national monuments, so they'd be ideal for an action adventure or even a mystery that unfolds with the discovery of ancient artefacts buried in one of the caverns.

Italian Splendour

Name: Dolomites

Geographical Area: Italy

Brief Description: Forming a part of the Southern Limestone Alps, the Dolomites are situated in northeastern Italy, spreading from the River Adige in the west to the Piave di Cadore Valley in the east.

USP: If you need your characters to experience Italian beauty, they won't go wrong travelling between the provinces of Belluno, South Tyrol. and Trentino.

The area looks very Swiss, so you also have the option to make up a fictional location with some elements of Italy's splendour and other locations that would suit your premise.

Valley of The Moon

Name: Valle de la Luna

Geographical Area: San Pedro de Atacama, Chile

Brief Description: This exceptional 'Valley of the Moon' is one of the most visited places in San Pedro. Located near San Pedro, it has stones and sand formations (carved by wind and water) that resemble the surface of the moon, with colours and textures of the desert. A prototype for a Mars rover was tested there by scientists because of the valley's dry and forbidding terrains

USP: The dry lakes leave a layer of salt and diverse saline outcrops, giving it an appearance of man-made sculptures. There are also a great variety of caverns, making it ideal for a fantasy world setting or science fiction. The valley is considered one of the driest places on earth because some areas have not received a single drop of rain in hundreds of years, so this could be a dystopia setting.

6 Mighty Mountains; Keep on Climbing

Mountain scenes are spectacular and can be used in just about any genre. Sure, some genres are more suitable than others, but give your mind a wide berth when it comes to mountains and valleys. Both can be scary for your POV or just the opposite. Use your bubbling pot to sift through ideas for how your character can come a cropper in one of these areas.

More Setting Ideas

Get your character thinking about these places: A rough track down a valley, a bumpy and uneven mountain path, a narrow crevice on the side of a mountain or a desolate shack amidst the trees.

Scary and Spooky

Mansions, castles, underground railways (see Down Below), whatever will terrify a reader.

Eerie Lighthouse

Name: St Augustine Lighthouse

Geographical Area: Florida, United States

Brief Description: St. Augustine Lighthouse is located in the northern end of Anastasia Island, in St. Augustine, Florida. The impressive lighthouse was built in 1874. Throughout its history, St. Augustine Lighthouse has been the home of many keepers. However, in 1955 lighthouses became automated, so there was no longer a need for keepers or assistants to live inside the structure. St. Augustine Lighthouse became famous all around the United States when it was featured in an episode of *Ghost Hunters*. It's believed that seven people died inside this lighthouse: three keepers, a keeper's wife and three young girls. USP: If you want to totally isolate your characters, an abandoned lighthouse is a good way to get them alone and scared out of their wits.

Mood Details

Mood: Dark and scary at night or in a storm, and spooky if haunted.

Colours: the blue of the sky meeting the ocean's tranquil green on a clear day or turbulent dark watery depths in a storm.

Both can be used to convey the mood and atmosphere of a thriller, crime scene or haunted story.

Weather: Rough, stormy weather contrasted by calm seas. You could use tides as a plot thread; maybe your hero arrives during low tide, but things go against him when the tide sneaks up and isolates him, leaving him alone with the ghost of a lighthouse-keeper. Use elements such as rain driving against and into doors, standing water on sills, and interior condensation.

Visual: Bright red and black lighthouse towering into an indigo sky, set against a turquoise sea and grass green cliff banks. If your lighthouse is in England, use the chalky-white cliffs of Dover.

Item Details

Ground: Rocks surround a lighthouse; some have sheer cliffs; others may be out at sea or set into a sandy beach

Ceiling: Endless skies which change mood with the weather. The top of the lighthouse (the light room) is constructed mainly of cast-iron with copper and brass fittings.

Walls: Lighthouses could be hemmed in with stone walls or wide open to the elements.

Doors: Lighthouse doors could be creaky, watertight sheet-iron or tongue-and-groove wooden planks. Many entrances are detailed with large raised panel doors trimmed with masonry or cast-iron pediments and pilasters.

Props: Ropes, anchor, life raft, life buoy, fishing nets, reflector bulbs, lamp-changer, radiant optic lights with flashing or revolving apparatus, fog horn. Does your lighthouse have communication devices such as a radio?

Not if you want to isolate your heroine. Is the lighthouse equipped to have someone living in it? It may have no furniture if it's completely abandoned.

You could add a bed, a chair, a table, maybe the odd tin of food if your character is being held a prisoner. There'll be no running water, no electricity, no heating.

Obstacles: Slippery rocks, high cliffs, crossing beach, incoming tides, light going out.

Plants: Brambles climbing the cliffs; in an abandoned lighthouse weeds could web the doorways.

Animals: Spider webs trailing the iron stairs, rats scurrying into crevices, seagulls nesting, owls hooting in the tall pines. Maybe your lighthouse is surrounded by a Kelp Forest (seaweed), or treacherous reefs.

General Details

Backstory: Features include functional and decorative architecture such as steps, balustrades, pilasters, and architraves.

Genre or Type of Scene: Good for fight scenes or isolating a character. Ideal for thrillers, crime or horror. Could be a contrast such as horror mixed with love. Two lovers might find themselves breaking into the lighthouse one night, looking to create unforgettable memories, while being closely watched and taunted by a twisted stranger. Or the keeper ghost.

People Details

People: People who don't mind the solitary isolation would live here, probably a keeper and his wife or just him and his dog.

Family or non-family friendly: A keeper may have kids to add more plot threads to your story.

If your story demands a working lighthouse, you'll need staff operating the lighthouse and discussing daily work matters. A grumpy lighthouse keeper could be a lovely character to create.

Sensory Details

Sights: The bright revolving light at night, the endless view out to sea, a sharp rock jutting out of the roiling sea like someone trying to escape drowning. If haunted, maybe a large, dark male appears in the basement, possibly the spirit of a former caretaker who hung himself in the lighthouse when his wife left. Moving shadows and an unseen presence.

Smells: Dank and mouldy interior, a hint of the ocean mixed with an overbearing metallic tang of iodine and rotting fish lying in puddles of water, a sharp odour of oil in the basement amongst the light equipment, the rancid scent of copper rising from long-standing rusting apparatus.

Taste: Salty waves thrashing against the rocks, boiled cabbage, tinned fish.

Touch: Slimy, clammy, damp, wet, cold, smooth, slippery.

Sounds: Waves crashing onto the rocks, creaking wooden stairs, metal grinding and squeaking in the old abandoned automated tower, squawking seagulls. For a haunting, try footsteps shuffling on the gravel or thumping up the steps at night. The suggestion of someone climbing the tower steps, walking through the lighthouse or even tinkering with the old traditional lighting system. If your lighthouse is out at sea, the sounds of waves crashing against the rocks and into the tower can be frightening, especially if a character is alone and isolated.

Other Notes

For many sailors, the lighthouse was the light at the end of the sea's tunnel. You may want to peep at Owl's Head Lighthouse, which is in Maine, because it's said to be one of the most well-known haunted lighthouses in the United States. Your lighthouse could be on the rocks out at sea, but you have to find a way to get your characters there. Or it could be on the rocky cliff's edge. Maybe the cliff is crumbling, like many coastal cliffs, which could give lots of story angles.

You could have your character go and live there for historic research or to renovate the lighthouse. Perhaps he finds a keeper's notebook. Then, maybe he hears mysterious pacing sounds upstairs, which indicates that the keeper still tends his beloved lighthouse.

Now Your Turn

As with settings down below, if one of these places triggers some ideas, either find a way to use them or adapt them as necessary.

Fire Storm

Name: Burnt Out Building

Geographical Area: Ladbroke Grove, London

Brief Description: Fireplace with fire-singed floorboards. Large light minimalist house with unique burnt-out top rooms. Burnt out furniture and props.

USP: If you've read my book in my Writer's Resource Series called *A~ Z of Behaviours, Foibles, Habits, Mannerisms & Quirks for Writers to Create Fictional Characters,* then you'll have read about the fire-player. This setting could be the home that he set on fire, either his or the heroine's home. Great for a crime thriller.

Red River

Name: Rio Tinto

Geographical Area: Spain

Brief Description: This 'red river' with its alien-lunar-like landscape runs from the spectacular Sierra Moreno Mountains down to the Gulf of Cádiz in historic Huelva. Its red colouring is due to the high level of iron in its waters. From ancient times the river has been mined for copper, gold and silver. Fabled to be King Solomon's mine, the Rio Tinto is believed to be the oldest mine in the world. With all the mining going on in the river, it has a high acidic content that is home to organisms that survive in extreme conditions.

USP: Scientific studies of the river, similar to those conducted in the underground lakes of Mars and Jupiter, could be what your characters are here to do. What they find, and what they do about it, could be your alien adventure.

Ghost Town

Name: Bodie

Geographical Area: California

Brief Description: One of America's famous ghost towns, Bodie once boasted two thousand buildings and a population of seven thousand.

The main street flourished with sixty-five saloons along the bustling mile. But as the mining industry went into decline, the town emptied and became a ghost town by the 1940s. It is now a National Historic Landmark run by California's State Parks.

USP: If you're writing a ghost story, you could use part of this town as your own setting or write a historical novel with all the true facts of what happened to these people.

Leap to Death

Name: Leap Castle

Geographical Area: Ireland

Brief Description: Although Dracula's Playground is said to be in a creepy and remote corner of the Carpathian Mountains in Romania, where Bran Castle sits high upon craggy peaks within Transylvania, there's no historic proof that Vlad the Impaler resided in Dracula's Castle during his reign of terror. So, instead of Romania, we'll leap to Ireland to the most haunted Celtic castle. Legend has it that more than four hundred years ago, in 1532, brother turned against brother to shed blood. One was a warrior who rushed into the chapel and used his sword to slay the priest who was his brother. The priest fell across the altar and died. The chapel has been known as Bloody Chapel ever since.

USP: If you're writing a horror or historical novel, you'll want to explore the dungeon in this castle. Prisoners pushed through the trap door of the oubliette fell eight feet onto spikes coming up from the floor. Leap Castle is also haunted by an Elemental, a dark evil creature about the size of a sheep, with a human face and black pools for eyes. It smells of rotting flesh. Alternatively, it's a great place to go for a ghost hunt, but maybe not a comedy.

Ring of Stones

Name: Stonehenge

Geographical Area:

Brief Description: Stonehenge is a prehistoric monument located in Wiltshire, England, between Amesbury and Salisbury.

Undoubtedly one of the most famous sites in the world, Stonehenge is the ruins of a ring of standing stones set in the middle of a complex of Neolithic and Bronze Age monuments. Although archaeologists believe it was constructed around 3000 BC, radiocarbon dating suggests the first bluestones were raised between 2400 and 2200 BC, and that the deposits contain human bone.

USP: Does your character work for English Heritage or the National Trust and get caught up in some new findings? What are they? That aliens built this stone monument?

6 Scary Scenarios; What Else is Waiting for You?

Any place can be frightening if your villain is closing in on your POV. Use your mood details to create a dark and foreboding setting.

Search for scary places in the country your story takes place or add keywords for your genre and storyline to find more exceptional settings.

More Setting Ideas

Will you place your character in one of these setttings?

A rundown mansion, a forest or wood in the dead of night, a graveyard on the edge of town, an unused hospital or psychiatric ward, lost in a tube tunnel, on a deserted street or in a vacant playground.

Seascapes

These could also be treasure troves, lighthouses or sunken ships, and homes jutting out from the edge of a cliff.

Oyster Garden

Name: Chesapeake Oyster Bay

Geographical Area: Maryland

Brief Description: While oysters, sub-tidal snacks eaten both cooked and raw, are rumored to be a natural aphrodisiac, they can be unsanitary when taken straight from the sea.

So, after being harvested, the oysters are taken to an 'oyster garden' where they are cleaned. The oyster gardeners allow clean water to flow over the oysters, removing any impurities that they may have picked up from the ocean. After being cleaned in the garden, the oysters are then shipped around the world.

USP: Maybe your character falls in love with someone who cultivates oysters or someone who works in an oyster farm. Possibly the oyster expert is trying it on with your heroine and uses oysters to turn the tide in his favour.

Alternatively, you may want to have some kinds of pearl oysters being harvested for the pearl produced inside. Your storyline could be an innocent person picking up a decorative shell and discovering the world's most precious treasure inside. What would that be? What does she do with it? And how does she stop the baddies snatching it from her?

Mood Details

Mood: Fishy and watery.

Colours: The sun dazzles the water, bright sparkles of sun dance on the water. After sunset the water becomes a dark, brooding mass. Your heroine will quickly be amazed at the kaleidoscope of watercolours of the oyster shell, ranging from purple, to green, and even a soft shade of pink.

Weather: Sea storms whip up quickly. Clouds will make the gardens shadowy and gloomy. Bright sun can cause headaches.

Visual: Hatches of oysters in watery caged baskets.

Item Details

Ground: Watery cages house the oysters being cleaned or cultivated.

Ceiling: Endless skies, either azure blue or stormy steel grey.

Walls: Cages for the oysters could see your character 'walled in' if you're writing a thriller; that's if your villain is crafty enough to stuff your heroine inside one.

Doors: The gardens are wide open on sandy shores and water inlets.

Props: Wooden jetty and docks, oyster cages, mesh wire, water buckets, life buoy suits, algae, seaweed, shrimp, rotting crab shells, piles of empty oyster shells.

Obstacles: Ebb tides and flood tides, as well as any of the props.

Plants: Seaweed strewn across the beach, sprawled up against the rock pools and rotting in the sun over dry oyster cages.

Animals: Zooplankton, the animal form of plankton, crabs, shrimp, fishing bait, oysters and seagulls.

General Details

Backstory: The Chesapeake Bay Foundation's Oyster Gardening Program gives people the opportunity to help bring back this vital species by growing oysters alongside their docks. Once grown, the adult oysters are returned to the Chesapeake Bay Foundation for planting on sanctuary reefs. They say oysters can be grown from a private dock, community pier, marina, waterfront business, or a friend or neighbour's dock.

Genre or Scene Type: This is a great place for a children's or young adult story. It would be just as exciting to stage a romance here, but then a thriller, mystery, romance, or children's and young adult horror would also work.

People Details

People: Lots of families come to this oyster garden to help revive the oyster population.

Family or non-family friendly: This particular oyster garden encourages children and young people to get involved with reviving the oyster population.

Sensory Details

Sights: People clinging to the wooden jetty, hanging in the radiant water as they tend to their oyster cages.

Smells: A slightly fishy oyster smell hangs in the air, mingled with the briny smell of the sea. There may be the sharp tang of lemon squeezed over the oysters that clears the air a bit. Bad oysters have a strong, offensive, or pungent fishy smell.

Taste: The brackish water will be salty and taste of brine. Eating raw or undercooked oysters can be dangerous and make your character ill pretty quickly. Fresh oysters can be crisp and crunchy or firm and slippery as they slide down the throat. Some oysters can be a salt overload; that's why the shock of lemon gives a fresh citrus tang. Some oysters may have a very strong, acidic or rusty flavour.

Touch: Winds in the bay can pick up quickly and whip the beach sand across your legs and hands, so your character will feel a gritty, stinging sensation. The freshest, best quality oysters should have a buttery, creamy texture and feel squashy to touch.

Sounds: Seagulls squabbling over a piece of loose oyster flesh. Families jabbering with excited yells from kids. The occasional twang of mesh on an oyster cage or a thunk as it splashes into the bay.

Now Your Turn

The sea is a vast expanse of scene-setting opportunities. Any of these could so easily be mixed up to create your comedy, love story or scary novel with the ocean, calm and serene or wild and stormy, as your back drop.

The Sea God

Name: Bell Rock Lighthouse

Geographical Area: Scotland

Brief Description: Built between 1807 and 1810 on the Bell Rock (also known as Inchcape) in the North Sea, this lighthouse was constructed to such a high standard that it has not been replaced or adapted in 200 years.

It is out at sea, 11 miles east of the Firth of Tay, and rises 35 metres above the ocean with its light being visible from 35 miles inland.

USP: As this is the world's oldest surviving sea-washed lighthouse, it definitely deserves to be the scene of an action adventure, a ghost story or part of a thriller.

Suspended Lake

Name: Lake hanging over the sea

Geographical Area: Faroe Island, Denmark

Brief Description: The tranquillity of the Faroe Islands is what makes so many city slickers want to escape their city madness. They visit to enjoy the fantastic scenery, when the islands turn an extraordinarily shade of green during the summertime. Without knowing what you have in store for them, your character comes here for the fresh air, the deep blue ocean, the vertical sea cliffs and the green mountains with their picturesque valleys. USP: With the incredible lake literally hanging over sea, maybe your hero is a rock climber with a group of adventurous friends determined to scale the impossible cliff up to the lake. When the summer fog creates a mystical landscape, do they go ahead or not? Are they mad enough?

The lake is surrounded by a higher precipice, which prevents it from emptying into the ocean. The water exit is the waterfall Bøsdalafossur. With or without risky rock climbers, these islands give you a fabulous setting with lots of history and mystical stories to create your own historic novel or fantasy story. Or any other genre, for that matter.

Atlantis is Found

Name: Underwater sculpture park

Geographical Area: Mexico

Brief Description: For centuries explorers have searched for the lost city of Atlantis. Many a tale has been written about the fictional discovery of the watery city.

USP: So if your characters stumble on this park in Mexico, they would be forgiven for thinking they had found an ancient citadel lost to the seas. But maybe this artificial reef, decorated with manmade sculptures, is hiding something real. Will your diving group discover a sunken treasure, and reveal the true and correct location of the real Atlantis? With fiction, anything is possible; that's why we love to write!

Raising Giants

Name: Giant's Causeway

Geographical Area: Northern Ireland

Brief Description: Ireland is a beautiful place with wonderfully friendly people. Of course I would say this when my husband is Irish, but I found this out long before I met him. It may not be the most obvious place for your character to enjoy an adventurous romp or be chased by villains, but why not? Just Google for the best places in Ireland to find out how you could use the basalt rock formations on the northern coast and so many other settings in this stunning country.

USP: Sixty million years ago a huge volcanic eruption spewed out a mass of molten basalt, which then solidified and contracted as it cooled, creating the cracks that can be seen today. Forget the Scottish Highlands for your romance and send your marine biologist couple to the Giant's Causeway in Ireland. Here he'll explore or examine the results of the ancient volcanic eruption that now features some 40,000 hexagonal basalt columns. If the idea of a romantic tale sickens you, crime, horror and even comedy would do just as well here. Or maybe you'll prove the historians and geologists wrong and create a fantasy about the giants who really built this causeway to their colossal castle along the shore.

Salt Mirror

Name: Salt flats

Geographical Area: Bolivia

Brief Description: Some of the places I have found for this book don't seem to belong to this world, and would be ideal for creating a new world, which I am now inspired to do. This is one of them.

These salt flats are inhospitable and bizarre. In the rainy season, fresh water creates a mirror effect spreading along the flats, giving the impression that you're driving across a lake.

USP: Situated at an altitude of almost four thousand metres above sea level, salt is not the only element your characters will find; there'll be snow and ice when the temperature dips below zero. Are they travelling or on safari? Or are they scientists testing something that happened on the other side of the world, but relates back to their own location?

Devil's Triangle

Name: The Bermuda Triangle

Geographical Area: North Atlantic Ocean

Brief Description: Long shrouded in myth and mystery, the infamous 500,000 square miles also dubbed the Devil's Triangle is roughly the area between Bermuda, Florida and Puerto Rico.

USP: Although the US Coastguard disputes any such area exists, conspiracy theories thrive on stories about unusual magnetic readings and ships, planes and people who have disappeared here without a trace. So it seems the ideal place to rock your character's boat and set him afloat with conflict. Could it be a time warp story, or a futuristic tale? Science fiction, time travel, aliens, supernatural, nautical thrillers all would 'go down' well here.

Red Tide

Name: Red Beach, Panjin

Geographical Area: China

Brief Description: I love the weird places I have encountered on this journey of mine to find 101 settings.

This one is totally bizarre because this beach is covered in a type of seaweed called Sueda, which turns bright red in autumn. Thirty kilometres southwest of Panjin, these tidal wetlands are an important nature reserve for migrating birds. Only a small section of the beach is open to the public, but it can be explored via a wooden walkway that stretches out to sea.

USP: Anything could happen here: a love story where locals meet to see the phenomena, a thriller where this seaweed is causing a sea-borne virus, a crime where the killer hides the bodies in the wetlands and the seaweed eats them up, aliens coming down to feed on this seaweed to become more human ... I could go on and on, but hopefully something has sparked in your bubbling pot and will fester and fizzle to create your own red tide.

8 Oceanic Berths; You're Just Getting Your Feet Wet!

The ocean needs a lot of respect; of that we are certain. So if your character is dicing with death near any large body of water, there are stacks of ideas for putting them in peril. Alternatively, your story could be a children's adventure or romance near a river. Check out the world's best beaches, seascapes, sea pictures or most turbulent oceans. Take a punt on nautical vehicles like boats, submarines, oil rigs or cruise lines, even river barges may work. They're on the water, after all. Search for your story premise and add a + for any other keywords. Make your POV scared of water or unable to swim. At junior school one of my classmates itched when water touched her skin. Imagine someone's life without water!

More Setting Ideas

These additional ideas may jostle an idea for a seascape setting: sunken ship, smuggler's inn, a cave along the seashore, a secluded cove, an isolated beach, rock pools, a beach café or a remote island.

Tight and Narrow

These places are ideal for placing the hero in a tight spot where he has to work out how to get out.

The Heart of India

Name: Chandni Chowk

Geographical Area: Old Delhi, India

Brief Description: Chandni Chowk's is known for the variety of its markets and their Indian-specific products: from authentic Indian food, delicacies and sweets of more than 1,000 varieties, to sarees with beautiful chikan and zari work. The market is full of narrow lanes with shops selling books, clothing, shoes and leather goods, electronic and consumer goods and anything you can imagine. The area, even more so than the rest of the city, is very congested.

USP: Built in the 17th century, this is one of the oldest and busiest markets in India; this setting could be of interest to anyone from a political escapee to an archeologist on the hunt for Indian treasures to a drug lord or even a tourist falling in love with their Indian travel guide.

Mood Details

Mood: Heavy, suffocating, crowded.

Colours: All colours are present in this landscape, but dominated by browns, orange, autumnal colours from the city buildings contrasted with vivid greens and reds from the women's clothing.

Weather: Sunny, hot, the skin is moist and sweaty.

Visual: The jalebis, a particular local delicacy, are fried in pure ghee.

Simile or Metaphor: Looks like a place where all cultures of the world collide. Smells like an old Indian home, filled with spicy food and home-made sweets.

Item Details

Ground: The cracked stone ground is a reminder that this market was built in the 17th century and that billions have walked its streets.

Ceiling: The market buildings' roofs are tiled and low

Walls: Many of the town walls are made of brick and possibly even stone

Doors: Lots of doors lead off the busy market and town square; they are primarily wooden, and some are rickety and falling apart.

Props: Hundreds of products on sale in the market, most importantly the traditional Indian items and not high-end boutiques.

Obstacles: Street vendors, market stalls, bicycles, fruit and veg baskets, too many people.

Plants: Only in places where plants are sold, so not much greenery.

Animals: A pack of stray dogs may run across the market, from bin to bin, in search of the first meal for this day. Puppies and adult canines alike are famished and rush to find relief in the food people throw away. Luckily, the market is full of restaurants and bins are full at this time of day.

General Details

Backstory: Chandni Chowk, or the Moonlight Square, was designed and established by Princess Jahanara, Shah Jahan's favourite daughter, in 1650 CE.

Genre or Type of Scene: Fight scenes, with eluding the attacker, or maybe setting a trap for him; thriller, mystery, adventure.

People details

People: Dressed in typical Indian clothes, the workers of the market are humble and kind. You can see in their dark, beautiful, yet hopeful eyes that life hasn't been easy on them. Family is the most precious thing and this is what they talk about with each other. When talking to outsiders, you can see the pride the people take when discussing Indian culture, and the spark in their eyes when somebody opens up and talks about the world outside the market. For most of them, the only way they get to know what is outside Old Delhi is through the tourists.

Family or non-family friendly: Family friendly

Sensory Details

Sights: Vivid colors, motion, traffic, pedestrians, crowded and rushed, so much happening at once.

Smells: Spicy food, chili spattering in pans, rotting fruit by the wayside, dry curry spices being blended by stall vendors

Taste: Hot curry spices set the heart racing as they burn the taste buds and produce beads of sweat on the brow.

Touch: Soft fabrics such as silk.

Sounds: Loud chatter, car horns, bicycle bells, vendors shouting, children playing, dogs barking

Now Your Turn

With one full list above, go through the list below and create your own from any of these places that inspire you. Remember to copy and paste or download the list so you can work up your own scene settings.

From the ideas below, add any other details you can think of, especially sensory details.

Coffee Stop

Name: Coffee Shoppe

Geographical Area: Fulham, London

Brief Description: This unusual coffee shop has a seating area and large workspace with a long counter where your crime scene could take place. Possibly even use this as a fight scene where there are lots of props such as hot drinks and crockery that the hero could smash over the villain's head, after he drags him along the counter.

USP: Tight and narrow space that could work well for a fight scene, a quiet romantic meet-up or a trading place for someone to pass info to a mysterious stranger. Fulham also has a footballing history that could tie into your story.

Homing in Hong Kong

Name: Homes in Hong Kong

Geographical Area: Hong Kong

Brief Description: Coping with moving about in tiny homes is part and parcel of living in Hong Kong.

A family of four commonly lives in a flat of less than 50 square metres. Some families even cram into tiny apartments that are subdivided into cubicles. Poorer people rent cage homes, which is a wire mesh cage that can only fit a thin mattress stacked on top of another. Needless to say, this kind of living poses health and safety risks. When my husband lived there many years ago, some families even used under the stairs or the balcony for a bedroom for their maids.

USP: With that in mind, could it be that your character lands in Hong Kong to seek out a lead in a mystery and has to search through this bevy of bodies? Or perhaps he gets entangled in a terror threat with a virus victim let loose. Will he find that carrier before the entire city is infected?

Traffic Stopper

Name: Smallest home in Toronto

Geographical Area: Toronto, Canada

Brief Description: The land on which the house sits was originally designed as an alley for one of the neighbouring homes. City officials never approved the curb cut, so in 1912, contractor Arthur Weeden decided to make use of the land and built a house on it where he and his wife lived for 20 years.

USP: With only 312 sq. ft. of space, the Little House is a neighbourhood favourite, and stops traffic from time to time. Okay, with the cost of living so high, we know more and more younger couples are down-sizing and smaller living is in vogue. What if your character lived sandwiched between two neighbours, yet hated being near people or hated hearing his neighbours?

Denser Than Dense

Name: Narrow Home

Geographical Area: Brazil

Brief Description: Brazilian Heneita Minho lives in the narrowest house in the world. She designed and built a three-story home a metre wide by ten metres tall. It's so narrow she cannot fully extend her arms when she walks in the front door. That said, it's a fully functioning home with two living rooms, a kitchen, three bedrooms with washrooms, and a veranda.

USP: Could your character be an architect coming to see how this untrained lady built her home and get caught up in a Brazilian drama? Whatever you do, just don't have her go up, because there's no place to escape.

5 Constricted Cavities; Now Fill in the Holes

Famous bridges or sports stadiums are also good places to constrict your hero. Depending on your premise, try searching for places that would suit that genre. Once you have found your setting, you can also use Google Maps to hone in on places where you could add more troubles.

Remember, if you're using a real location, find local places in that surrounding area to add depth to your setting. Research the place's name + interesting facts.

More Setting Ideas

How about these?

Tunnels or under road crossings, between houses, playground pipes, paths along the side of mountains, bridges over gullies, ventilation shafts, packed public transport or kids' playpark equipment during the after school rush.

You may want to consider scene possibilities in small spaces, such as trains, planes, trucks, buses and boats. They could be crowded with people and luggage or empty without passengers except your poor character who walks into a trap.

Another idea is to place your character in the vicinity of the narrow canals in Holland. Up north there are several villages connected by the canals. When they freeze over, it becomes a carnival skating rink for extreme ice-skaters who skate for miles from village to village. Let your imagination run wild with what could happen in those narrow frozen canals! Brrrr ...

Unusual Fight Scenes

Stunning places where the villain and hero clash.

Land Meets Sea

Name: Egremni Beach

Geographical Area: Greece

Brief Description: The beach is accessed from the car park via 347 steep steps that hug a rugged cliff that is a hundred and fifty metres high.

USP: If you use this as a fight scene in your Greek tale your character will not be able to escape easily. Make your heroine unfit so she gets out of breath charging up these stairs. Find rocks and natural obstacles for her to use as weapons in self-defence. Maybe your hero grapples the robber and saves the day.

Mood Details

Mood: Peaceful, sunny, light.

Colours: Blue, green and white are the predominant colours of this landscape. Your observant heroine will also notice the great variety of colours in the clothes the tourists are wearing because they come from all parts of the world to enjoy the sun and sand and sea.

Weather: Sunny, hot, dry.

Visual: The view from the top of the stairs is breath-taking.

Item Details

Ground: The beach is composed of fine to medium-sized pebbles that are very comfortable to lie on, in the white colour typical of the Ionian Islands.

Ceiling: Endless blue skies.

Walls: The stone cliff wall is covered in wild plants.

Doors: No physical doors, just the imaginary door to your romantic saga.

Props: Sand, stones, sea water, tourist backpacks, sunbathing creams.

Obstacles: Very difficult to climb the 300 plus stairs.

Plants: Wild plants grow spontaneously on the cliff.

Animals: Fish and birds and sea gulls.

General Details

Backstory: The waters of Egremni are clear and the sunsets are dramatic. Following the deadly earthquake that struck the Ionian island of Lefkada, killing two women, the entire landscape of the area has changed. The remote beach was sealed off in the mid-nineties and became one of the premier tourist destinations on the island for sunbathers.

Genre or Type of Scene: Fight scene for pirate adventure or conspiracy thriller, or just a sweet romance.

People details

People: Tourists

Family/non-family friendly: Both, and an idyllic place to take the kids for a family holiday if you can brace the stairs.

Sensory Details

Sights: Deep blue sea meeting equally blue skies with only a strip of golden sand alongside the rocky cliffs.

Smells: Salty sea air, a mix of perfumed and sultry sun creams, exotic ice cream with the overwhelming scent of fresh fruit.

Taste: Salty and sandy sandwiches gone crusty in the sun or soggy in the heat. Tangy fruit ripening and softening in the fierce sun, sweet orange juice refreshers.

Touch: Smooth pebbles, grainy sand, salty sea, sweaty palms, dry beach towels, soggy wet costumes filled with sand.

Sounds: Tourists enjoying themselves, seagulls crying out for the odd breadcrumb, children playing, waves splashing onto the shore.

Other Notes

Although idyllic for a family, maybe your characters are caught in a location similar to this when a giant wave explodes onto the beach after a mad scientist out at sea sets off an off-shore earthquake. Could he be so cruel as to close the stairs to see what happens when hundreds of people are trying to escape at once? Will the stairs stand the stampede?

Now Your Turn

Remember that any of the settings listed in this book could be a fabulous location for your fight scene.

From the underwater worlds to the mountains or homes and offices. Just imagine your hero and villain facing each other with swords or knives or no weapon on the volcano-like entrance to the Russian diamond mine. Let your imagination run wild when you come to look for a fight setting. And you must read Rayne Hall's book on how to write fight scenes; I couldn't write one without it!

Red Boat Studio

Name: Recording Studio Boat

Geographical Area: Canning Town, London

Brief Description: A unique recording studio on a boat moored along the Thames. Along with a traditional fire stove, a log fire heats its huge iron hull. Porthole windows above a modern kitchen bring in natural river light. Best feature is the super huge and roomy recording studio.

USP: Your crime novel, mystery or romance character could have an adventurous romp above or below deck. All the expensive recording kit could be used as natural defence weapons in a fight scene.

Mars Look-Alike

Name: Goblin Valley State Park

Geographical Area: Utah, USA

Brief Description: While it may look like Mars or another alien location, this valley, with more than two hundred miles of soft sandstone, is close to Salt Lake City. Eroded by wind and water, it has strange pinnacles and bizarre formations that resemble goblins, thus making the landscape eerie.

USP: If you're into action adventure this is a good place to have your fight scene. How and where your characters fight in this vast place is up to you. Or maybe your character is a world-renowned climber determined to scale these goblin peaks, but gets hoodwinked instead.

Library Masterpiece

Name: The Library of Trinity College

Geographical Area: Dublin

Brief Description: As the largest library in Ireland and, as a legal 'copyright library,' the Library of Trinity College has rights to receive material published in the Republic of Ireland free of charge; it is also the only Irish library to hold such rights for the United Kingdom. The library is an Irish masterpiece and is one of Ireland's biggest tourist attractions. It provides a home to thousands of rare and very early volumes. The Book of Kells is located in the Old Library, along with the Book of Durrow, the Book of Howth and other ancient texts.

USP: Your character may be here studying old manuscripts or searching to find a piece of a mystery or conspiracy where she will spend time in The Long Room. You have to check my Pinterest board (http://bit.ly/21JDdLg) to see this magnificent room. It's the oldest of its kind in Ireland, dating back to 1712.

The 65-metre-long main chamber of the Old Library, the Long Room, houses 200,000 of the Library's oldest books. It's lined with marble busts from great Irish philosophers and writers.

I have to admit I feel terribly guilty for adding this stunning setting as a fight scene, but it would be so unique to have your villain and hero battle it out in this setting with old balustrades and stairways, high domed ceilings, and some of the world's most precious books to throw at each other. Ouch, what a devil I am to even suggest such an atrocity!

Iced Diamonds

Name: Mir Diamond Mine

Geographical Area: Mirny, Eastern Siberia, Russia

Brief Description: One of man's own creations, the former diamond mine in Russia has been inactive for 10 years.

USP: When your hero is sent to analyse the Mir diamond mine in Russia, he will be shocked. Not only is it the second largest excavated hole in the world, next to the Kimberley diamond mine, it's also covered in icy snow, and he'd need to be working in an area of over 1km. Imagine a fight scene on the brink of this hell hole?

5 Battle Grounds, but So Many More

Fights will take place anywhere, from a cosy intimate home or a manic office to any number of places the two clashing characters will find a reason to throw punches.

Find props in that setting for your characters to fall over, drop into, or hang from. And use the weather to make the contest even tougher for both protagonist and antagonist.

More Setting Ideas

Maybe your character would like to choose one of these settings to battle the villain: posh restaurant, packed warehouse, stinking animal barn filled with diseased sheep, broken scaffolding, scuba diving with faulty gear, busy station platform, airport queue, between Icelandic geysers, through a swamp, in a shark cage under water, or down a bobsleigh run.

Unusual Homes

Get inspired by these weird, way-out or simply horrid homes where heroes or villains live, such as a lighthouse, narrowboat house or world war bunker.

Underground Bunker Conversion

Name: Luxury Apartments

Geographical Area: Caversfield, near Bicester, Oxfordshire

Brief Description: From their origins as a decontamination bunker, these new homes have no windows, yet have a high market value in British Pounds.

USP: It may be an unusual home, but what about a young trendy couple moving in only to find their modern designs destroyed by a graffiti ghost who died in the bunker and hates to see it changed to such a happy environment?

Mood Details

Mood: Light and airy with highly modern interiors.

Colours: Outside, the red brick bunker wall is dominant, while the interior design is based on different shades of whites and creams, blended with warm browns.

Weather: Sunny in the summer and rainy for most of the year so the British climate lends a lot to spooky tales and ghostly stories where the weather plays a big role in scaring your readers.

Visual: You immediately notice the sign on the outer wall: 'The bunker.'

Item Details

Ground: Quiet to walk on wooden flooring and expensive Italian tiles.

Ceiling: The ceiling is V-shaped with windows carved into the ceiling, to allow as much light as possible into the former bunker.

Walls: In some parts the walls are only feet tall with a glass wall separating the living room and terrace. Thanks to this glass wall, light comes into the home to stop it from looking like a dark, dank, dreary war bunker.

Doors: The green entry doors are made of light wood with a glass door separating the living room from the terrace.

Props: Household appliances, furniture, knives – lots of them if you are thinking of a modern slasher story or a killer ghost.

Obstacles: The lack of windows will help to keep your heroine trapped when the killer comes at her with her favourite carving knife. Lots of glass for the villain to break and cut up his victims in a slasher novel.

Plants: Plants in pots and lawn in the front yard, all seemingly innocent, unless the neighbour is growing drugs and the heroine finds out.

Animals: Cute small pets would live happily in this home, unless the ghost lost his cat and feels revenge that the heroine's cat is still here in his bunker.

General Details

Backstory: Although these Second World War bunkers were built to withstand a bombing, gas or chemical attack, they now sport decontamination showers, air lock doors and a war room.

Genre or Type of Scene: Love scene or erotic setting amongst all the glass, family drama, ghost story, horror, slasher, thriller, time-slip war story or young adult mystery.

People details

People: The residents buying this home would be elegant, forward-thinking and modern individuals. Except the neighbour growing cannabis who may run a large drug ring in south London.

Family/non-family friendly: Family-friendly, until the kids start chewing on the strange plants the neighbour is growing.

Sensory Details

Sights: Although it's fronted by a gloomy brick-slab entrance, the windows on the ceiling are a great way to enhance lighting in the house and to catch your guests' attention.

Smells: It may smell of brand new leather, potpourri baskets and that lovely new polished smell.

Taste: Your POV would taste the subtle perfumed fragrance lingering in this home, until the sour tang of 'weed' assaults their nostrils.

Touch: Soft fabrics, cold glass table and surfaces, steel knives, spongy lounge suite, warm bed.

Sounds: The sound of children playing on the terrace, classical music to lift the mood, until the neighbour gets home and starts blasting out his heavy-metal. Or was that the ghost tormenting your heroine before the neighbour came home?

Other Notes

Although it looks like a museum on the outside, it's all warm and fuzzy on the inside. If you fancy a bunker as a home, office place or even your villain's lair, check this site: http://bit.ly/1VMyNML

Now Your Turn

There are so many whacky places your characters could live if it suits your storyline. Even if it doesn't, you can make them far more memorable to your reader by giving them a unique place to live. Show those personal and emotional details too. Would any of these work for you?

Pretty Belinda

Name: Boathouse Home

Geographical Area: Thames River, London

Brief Description: A high spec houseboat moored on the river Thames. Beautifully appointed throughout, the houseboat is spacious, stylish and bright. It features open plan living, dining kitchen, with separate snug. Ultra-mod bedrooms and bathrooms with great river views.

USP: You could hem your character in with this home or get her locked into the villain's home where the only avenue of escape is the dirty, swirling currents of the Thames.

Lofty Style

Name: Loft Home

Geographical Area: South Kensington, London

Brief Description: This unusual home or working office is a loft. Its working space is set over four floors and a walled garden, and it's packed with various styles of furniture and designer ideas ranging from the 1930s through to the present day.

USP: If your main character is an interior designer, she could be comfy in this way-out home, which could also be a setting for her office, until the villain comes along and sets it on fire with the heroine trapped in one of her eclectic designer rooms.

Modern Decay

Name: The House Next Door

Geographical Area: Stoke Newington, London

Brief Description: The house next door is a five floored former building for merchants situated on the corner of London's Jewish quarter. Wonderful textures and wallpapers adorn the walls. The house is served by large sash windows that provide great natural daylight and a number of differently themed rooms with varying colour schemes.

USP: If your main character is a photographer or works in the fashion industry, he'd be right at home here, until someone creaks along the original oak floorboards. Or as this home's name implies, your POV character could be spying on the house next door where all sorts of weird experiments are taking place.

Jet Stream

Name: Airstream Caravan

Geographical Area: Truro, Cornwall

Brief Description: Static airstream caravan set in a rural location overlooking a field of alpacas.

The remote setting could be ideal to isolate your heroine or keep them trapped. Or how about a romantic hideout for the bridegroom and bridesmaid before he marries her best friend? Might be good to hide a European Royal treasure in the surrounding fields, especially if it was first stolen off a high speed train travelling across Europe.

USP: Imagine your hero or villain needs a place to take cover. Where better than a rural hideout in Cornwall?

Hippie Hangout

Name: Narrowboat Home

Geographical Area: Paddington, London

Brief Description: This beautiful 45ft blue narrowboat features a large front deck, varnished wood interior, traditional decor and Morso squirrel solid fuel stove. It's currently moored in East London, but can be moved to any location on Regents canal, River Lea, Paddington Basin and Grand Union, Paddington.

USP: Another wonderful authentic home for your musical or hippie character to hang out. What if he came home one day to find his barge home on the move or disappeared completely? Would he find it, or trade it in for the musical artefact he's hiding? Would anyone even suspect a hippie living on a river boat to possess one of the world's greatest treasures?

6 Abodes; Keep Hunting

Okay, so you may not want your characters to live in a weird, way-out home; instead, choose something according to their careers, or something they can or can't afford to live in.

For your villain, you may want to devise a lair depending on what type of person he is, and what his plans are for the heroine. Whatever you choose, you can try searching for homes + genre + keywords that suit your story.

More Setting Ideas

Other ideas for character home settings could be a chapel, barge, river boat, loft house, communal camp or shared house community, high-rise studio and basement bedsit, flashy apartment, converted factory, lighthouse, war bunker, cabin in the woods, underground laboratory, converted church or a windmill.

Settings inside the home could be a bedroom, lounge, bathroom, shower room, wet room, attic, basement, cellar, dining room, kitchen, conservatory, play room, garage or a snug.

Close to home you could have junior and high schools, as well as universities or the village hall, kids' playgrounds, the local park, village shop or the village green.

Unusual Love Scenes

Where lovers could unite, tangle in each other's affairs and end up loving each other more than ever before.

Blooming Love

Name: Shinjuku Gyoen

Geographical Area: Shinjuku and Shibuya, Tokyo, Japan

Brief Description: Originally a residence of the Naitō family in the Edo period, it became a garden under the management of the Imperial Household Agency of Japan, and is now a park under the jurisdiction of the national Ministry of the Environment.

USP: The beautiful Shinjuku Gyoen National Garden is full of cherry trees, and is absolutely gorgeous in spring, so your love-birds would be delighted to sing to each other in your final romantic scenes.

Mood Details

Mood: Light, fun, romantic, full of life.

Colours: Green trees, blue ponds, pale pink cherry blossoms in abundant trees.

Weather: Hot and sunny.

Visual: Watching over 1500 cherry trees in bloom is quite a spectacle.

Simile or Metaphor: It's like all the beauty in the world emerges from the tips of these blooming cherry blossoms.

Item Details

Ground: Grass, soil, paved alleys, grassy banks for lovers to cuddle and get to know each other.

Ceiling: The greenhouse ceiling is made of glass and a metal framework with exotic plants growing inside.

Walls: Equally, the greenhouse walls are made of glass and metal framework. Makes me wonder if a fight scene could take place here amongst botanists creating a new creature-type-plant. I can imagine glass splintering and one of them sliding down the curved metal structure. Whoops, we're supposed to be in a romantic setting!

Doors: The doors are made of glass, but you could change that to gnarled old wood or broken bits of plastic if your plot demands other material to play with.

Props: Plants, flower pots, sticks, stones, water fountains.

Obstacles: Getting lost in such a big place is easy, pollen allergies are frustrating.

Plants: Various kinds of plants on exhibit, cherry trees outdoors, majestic Himalayan cedars, tulip trees, and cypress trees.

Animals: Squirrels, birds, and of course, the inevitable love-birds.

General Details

Backstory: While horticulturists have been working the grounds and greenhouses since 1892, the present greenhouse, built in the 1950s, has a stock of over 1,700 tropical and subtropical plant species on permanent display.

Genre or Scene Type: Romantic, where lovers can unite under a cherry tree while pink petals are falling from above. Too sickly sweet for you? Try a horror story to create a wild contrast, or maybe someone is creating air-borne viruses right under the cherry trees. Or perhaps supernatural forces are gaining strength with toxic plants. Why not crime, mystery or conspiracy too?

People details

People: Scientists, students, tourists, garden staff. Most come to this place because they enjoy nature.

Family/non-family friendly: Both, but lots of places for lovers to hide and canoodle.

Sensory Details

Sights: The mass of sprawled lovers lying on the pink carpet of petals is romantic, most have clasped hands or bodies spooned together.

Smells: The heady perfume of flowers floats over the lovers, with strong odours of cherry blossom and exotic scents oozing out of the indoor plant frame.

Taste: Many cuddling lovers may indulge in the setting and savour the sweet taste of cherries, accompanied by a buttery clotted cream.

Touch: Soft, humid touch of petals, spongy grass to lie on, a lover's rough tradesman hand caressing soft skin or a toxic plant eating through skin and bone. Ooh, sorry, what a horrible ending to our romance.

Sounds: Birds, squirrels, loving whispers and murmurs, that is, until the toxins arrive.

Now Your Turn

Love is always in the air, so any of the settings from the other categories will work well with a mix of comedy. Even spooky and scary stories have spoonsful of love thrown in here and there.

Erotic Temples

Name: Sun Temple at Konark and Maharashtra's Buddhist rock-cut monastic caves, Ajanta and Khajuraho in Madhya Pradesh

Geographical Area: India

Brief Description: While India is a conservative country, it appears that it wasn't always that way. Sexual norms were far more liberal before the 13th Century. Sex was taught as a subject in formal education, and Kamasutra, the world's first sex treatise, was written in ancient India between the 4th Century BCE and the 2nd Century CE. Graphic examples of erotic Indian art can be found carved in stone at the 13th Century Sun Temple at Konark in the east Indian state of Orissa. The same can be said of Maharashtra's Buddhist monastic caves, Ajanta, and the most erotic temple art can be found at Khajuraho in Madhya Pradesh. Temples are places of learning as well as worship, which seems to include the art of lovemaking. The portrayal of sexual actions may have been considered as a good omen, to symbolise new life.

USP: Looking closely, your character will see that most of these carvings are intensely erotic, and feature men, women and animals. There are depictions of threesomes and orgies. If your story is erotic, you may want your character in this setting at some point in your story. Maybe he's come to study these temples and their art. He probably won't be shocked by curvaceous young maidens and virile men twisting their bodies into impossible sexual positions.

Medicinal Soak

Name: Gangtey, Wangdue Phodrang

Geographical Area: Himalayan Kingdom of Bhutan

Brief Description: Nestled above a glacial valley is the 15th-century Gangtey Monastery, which will offer your character a scenic soak. It may only look like a farmer's stone shed, set in an open field planted with beetroot and potatoes, but this rustic bath is one of Bhutan's poshest spa resorts in the remote mountain-perched monasteries.

USP: Your heroine may not fall in love with the old smiling Bhutanese farmer wearing a traditional gho, a knee-length robe tied with a belt, but she may fall in love with his son who tends the farm, or a guide who takes her to this Bhutanese hot stone bath. Or possibly she's seeking the peace of the Buddhist way of life. She may be a travel agent creating a new luxurious journey, where guests stay in unique places like treehouses perched on a ridge, or holistic holidays offering a tour of all the hot stone baths in Bhutan. Maybe she is anti-medicine, but has an accident and meets a traditional Bhutanese doctor from the ancient 'Land of Medicinal Herbs.'

Living in a Fairy Tale

Name: Sopot Shopping Centre

Geographical Area: Poland

Brief Description: This zany *Alice in Wonderland* creation isn't a wall painting depicting a fairy tale book. The crooked house is actually real. Inspired by fairy tale books, this 4,000sqm building with its undulating roofline and warped windows and doors, houses a shopping centre, restaurants and a radio station. Its wackiness attracts thousands of tourists a year.

USP: Maybe your romantic character is really quirky (see my book on the *A~Z Writers' Character Quirks*) and built this house because she wants to live in a fairy tale. What if she meets someone just as eccentric? Or maybe a doctor has been sent by the family to put this person right, only to be sucked into this imaginative world.

Pink Lady Lake

Name: Hillier Lake

Geographical Area: Western Australia

Brief Description: If your character loves everything pink and fluffy, here's one for her. This pink lake is the only vividly pink lake she'll find in the world. Even when the water is removed to a separate container, it stays pink and never changes.

USP: Maybe your heroine who so loves pink is a scientist down under to find the mystery. She may or may not prove it's due to the presence of algae, unlike the other salt lakes down under, but can she explain to the world why it's pink? Or will that forever remain a mystery? Maybe the aboriginal guide she falls in love with has the secret, but when she meets their community and sees the startling results, she decides it's worth leaving the pink mystery intact.

5 Romantic Rendezvous Are Just the Beginning

If you need more inspiration, Google keywords like 'most romantic places in the world,' 'best romantic destinations,' 'top 10 most romantic places on earth' or words that suit your story such as honeymoon, wedding, cruise or couples retreat. Try the norm and then turn that on the head to find the opposite. For example, grand gardens, palaces, castles, Paris or Caribbean and then see what the opposite will be and more importantly, if it suits your romance. If you don't want your couple characters to be romantic, search for words that suit your genre and storyline and add 'places' or 'locations' on the end of a keyword string.

More Setting Ideas

Will your hero and heroine find love in one of these places: confession booth, crowded train carriage, scuba diving boat filled with tourists, a zoo, while undertaking adrenaline-spiked dangerous sports or simply in an igloo?

Unusual Work Places

This is a list of unusual places or buildings or areas where characters could work. Be inspired by these settings and use them for any plot setting, not just fancy work places for your fictional people.

Devil's Tower

Name: Devil's Tower

Geographical Area: Gulf of Mexico

Brief Description: Named after Devils Tower National Monument, Devil's Tower Oil Rig is located in the deepest water of the Mississippi Canyon region in the Gulf of Mexico.

USP: Metallic, other-worldly and alien, this tower could be a dystopic setting for your character who lives through a violent storm and crashes into the sea only to discover there's no one on the end of his SOS calls, and that the world has ended. Or you could create a fantasy water world or a science fiction setting.

Mood Details

Mood: Spooky, watery, high and risky.

Colours: The yellow painted oil platform is in harmony with the deep blue sea.

Weather: Humid, sweaty and sunny, but sea storms could raise havoc.

Visual: The red crane on the side of the oil platform stands out.

Item Details

Ground: The construction is immersed in water, with only sea for miles around.

Ceiling: The ceiling of the building has room for a helicopter, in case your character is a pilot.

Walls: The walls are built with heavy metal and iron.

Doors: Oil rigs have metal doors to ward off huge waves and bad weather.

Props: Equipment for drilling and maintenance aboard the platform, such as hammers and nail guns.

Obstacles: Sea sickness, being stranded on a platform in the middle of the gulf, and fear of heights could come into play, as well as the heavy oil rig tools.

Plants: Sea weeds tangling around the structure's metal legs and disappearing into the sea.

Animals: Plenty of fish and birds if your character can't find any food, but he'll need to dive in to catch them, or find old rusting spear guns.

General Details

Backstory: Originally built in 2003 by Dominion Exploration, which sold its Gulf of Mexico holdings to Eni, which now operates the platform.

Genre or Type of Scene: Good for fight scenes in a thriller or crime caper, also a horror, sea disaster or techno-thriller with this being the only safe place. Or maybe sea pirates use this as their base.

People details

People: Drill crew, well services crew, maintenance and supply workers. Or people from a fantasy or science fiction world.

Family/non-family friendly: Both, but I wouldn't want my kids running around this rusting structure, especially if they can't swim. If they grow up here and are like monkeys climbing around, well, that's different.

Sensory Details

Sights: The endless seascape can be breath-taking to a lover of the sea, but suffocating to a land-lubber. One glance at the ugly metal monstrosity rising out the azure depths could put you off a sea adventure.

Smells: Sea weed, rotting fish, thick wads of stinking black oil, diesel fumes, billows of smoke and intoxicating gas vapours.

Taste: Salty and pungent tang of fish guts, gusts of salty wind against the lips, oily quality that hangs in the air and leaves a revolting taste on the tongue.

Touch: Hot burning corrugated metal, slimy and slippery surfaces, hot steam, dust and dirt underfoot.

Sounds: Seagulls squawking, metal objects clanging, rush of thick, rich oil reserves, loud metallic banging noises, the sound of men yelling at each other, and the constant noise of the oil pump.

Other Notes

Although this oil platform is now owned by Williams Energy, you could use this setting as a real life location where your oil excavation manager gets caught up in a tangle, or it could be a completely fictional location in an ocean somewhere of your choosing. It looks like a giant alien robot, reaching its long iron arm (the crane) to pull out hidden oceanic treasures. Or maybe it's an alien monster lifting its iron baby eggs from the ocean floor.

Now Your Turn

When your character pops into your head, he may already have a place to work, but if not you could also get inspiration from resources on careers and jobs for your characters.

Holy House

Name: Camberwell Chapel

Geographical Area: Camberwell, London

Brief Description: The chapel has two mezzanines at opposite ends of the main building, providing full use of the huge ceiling height. Contemporary glass partitions and a sleek kitchen fit well into the space that has also retained many of its original structures. Features parquet flooring, stained glass, feature lighting, gallery library, design studio, outside space, baby grand piano, large Chinese carving and influences throughout.

USP: This magnificent arts-and-crafts style Chapel is a great place for a creative character to hang out. Its modern conversion could see a mystery unfold or those wonderful stained-glass windows could be shattered by a villain in a thriller. Shame to imagine that, but it could make a dramatic moment.

Aladdin's Industrial Cave

Name: MC Motors

Geographical Area: Dalston Kingsland, London

Brief Description: This Aladdin's cave industrial location oozes character and natural charm, with the sky windows providing an abundance of natural light. The warehouse has a chequered history with the largest room originally being part of the adjacent school whilst the rest was split into smaller industrial units. After the area was heavily bombed during the war the whole space was attached by the sky lighted roof, hence the untouched Victorian street running through the middle. Since then the building has been occupied by a boiler maintenance depot, the metropolitan water board, and most recently, a car mechanics shop.

USP: An odd assortment of character careers could take place in this industrial location, where your villain could be plotting all sorts of horrors.

Crowded Death Alley

Name: London Graveyard

Geographical Area: London

Brief Description: Let's face it, most of us, no matter what culture we come from, would prefer our final resting place to last for eternity.

The only problem is that in a city that has been inhabited for thousands of years, Londoners are quickly running out of space. This large cemetery has now started asking people if they would be willing to share their grave with a stranger.

USP: Could your serial killer be the cemetery manager who thinks he is pretty clever at hiding his victims? Maybe a poor family have to give in to the sharing policy and stumble upon the biggest body hoarding of the century. Will they simply just join the body sharing or will they find a way out?

Corpse Farm

Name: University of Tennessee

Geographical Area: Tennessee

Brief Description: Most farmers grow grain or raise cattle and sheep, but have you heard of anyone who runs a corpse farm? Better known as a forensic anthropology facility, this is where stiffs are laid in various states of decay, to assist student scientists and doctors in their studies. Sounds unbelievable, doesn't it? But the first corpse farm was started by the University of Tennessee in 1981 and began with just one corpse. Today this weird farm has over 40 corpses at any one time in a variety of states of decay. This increase in the number of bodies used on the farm has allowed forensic scientists greater advancements in their field.

USP: While your character could be one of these innocent students thinking she is studying natural decay, there could be a greater conspiracy wafting around the farm. If your hero owns a corpse farm, don't let him go bragging about his body count when he's had one too many down at the local pub. You never know who is listening to his ramblings. Great for crime or conspiracy, but could you also see a romance taking place amongst the students?

Smell Laboratory

Name: Rockefeller University

Geographical Area: New York

Brief Description: Depending on where we are and what we do, we open ourselves to pleasant and disgusting smells. From our body scents, to perfume or deodorant to the maddening smell of fresh bread lingering around our local supermarkets.

USP: What if the character in your romance story works in a smell laboratory producing synthetic scents and becomes oblivious to the smells around him, until one day the smell of a girl's Jasmine cologne suddenly awakens his senses?

6 Busy Bureaus as a Starting Point

This one is really dependent on the career of your character (or anyone in the story, for that matter). Look up different jobs, if one hasn't already sprung out at you, and then search for work places that suit that kind of employment. Also, try searching your storyline + most unusual careers or workplaces or offices or office buildings.

More Setting Ideas

Give your character a job in one of these places: laboratory, attic, basement, train, airplane, motorhome, nursery, pre-school, infant school, junior school, secondary school, college, Adult Education Centre, university, lecture theatre, research office, professor's office, staff room, evening classes, Sunday School classes, bible study, dentist room or morgue.

Up High

Risky scene settings way up high.

Kings Walk

Name: Caminito del Rey

Geographical Area: El Chorro Gorge, Spain

Brief Description: Caminito del Rey is by far the scariest path in the world with its narrow cliffside path hanging 100m above the waters of the river Guadalhorce. Meaning King's Little Path, the Caminito del Rey is built onto the side of the limestone rock face, and passes through the Desfiladero de los Gaitanes (Gaitanes Gorge) also known as Garganta del Chorro. The walkways offer spectacular, heart-stopping views down a sheer drop to the churning waters. The path runs from the Embalse de Guadalhorce reservoir through the famous El Chorro Gorge to El Chorro village, a major centre for rock-climbing. The nearest town Alora, is to the south along the Guadalhorce river valley.

USP: If you're writing about a pair of rock climbers who take risks for thrills, you definitely want them in Alora, a haven for rock climbing. Andalusia is characterized by large mountain ranges (and long gorgeous coastlines), making rock climbing a much-practiced sport throughout the many Sierras of this region.

Your characters will visit El Chorro, in Malaga, because there are hundreds of climbing routes. Nearby is Valle de Abdalajis and El Torcal, both exceptional mountains. With the rich Spanish culture, one or more of your climbing group should be Spanish.

Is it a love story of climbers falling for climbers (sorry!) or a thriller where one knows too much about something and decides to off his fellow climbers through 'accidents'? I may write this story one day because my Spanish home boasts this spectacular view down this valley with layers and layers of these stunning mountains, so I wouldn't have to go far to research this location. Besides, my hubby has done the walk and intends to take me up there soon. I am still holding my breath because I am determined to face my fear of heights!

Mood Details

Mood: Tense and breath-taking.

Colours: The biscuit coloured rock face slaps you in the face when you look at the steep walkway, but looking down gives you the soothing turquoise of the river meandering below.

Weather: Most of the year, this area has glorious sun. A few months will see rain and mist in between bright days, and on these days the walkway won't be open for visitors.

Visual: A sheer rock face, where walkers look like ants, that will scare the life out of anyone vaguely scared of heights.

Item Details

Ground: Solid rock all across the walkway with narrow metal railings for people to walk along the side of the cliff to enjoy the views.

Ceiling: In some parts you need to duck between one rocky path to another, but the rest is sky all the way.

Walls: Hemmed in with stone walls, some people even cling to the walls where the path is at its narrowest.

Doors: There are a few caves with dark shadowy entrances.

Props: Metal bars holding up the walkway, a sheer rock face up and down, lots of visitors ambling along.

Obstacles: Any of the props could be obstacles, some people even feel faint or get nauseous with the odd visitor throwing up over the edge.

Plants: Shrubs clings to the cliff face before you get to the main Kings Walkway, the rest of the way there is no vegetation along the cliffs, only wild brambles down below along the river valley.

Animals: Plenty of creatures creeping amongst the rocks with hawks flying high above the gorge looking for rabbits or mice down below. Bats reside in the caves, with rodents and reptiles aplenty.

General Details

Backstory: This three-kilometre-long cliff path is constructed with a wooded slatted boardwalk and a simple three-wire guard rail. In places it's only one-metre-wide, hanging onto the cliff face. Now, a new steel suspension bridge across the gorge beside the aqueduct bridge is a visitor highlight, but the original path can be seen just below the newly updated route, attracting thrill-seeking mountaineers from all over the world. Originally built around 1905 and improved around 1921, it fell into disrepair and over the past decades, the path became known as 'the most dangerous path in the world' and the 'walk of death.'

Genre or Scene Type: Your character would need to be adventurous and love taking risks to amble along here, unless the villain has threatened the heroine and forced her along for some reason; otherwise, the caves may be good for a mystery or horror. Or you could write up a story with the original history in mind.

People Details

People: Mostly tourists will visit this amazing location, but many locals enjoy taking friends to experience the walkway.

Family or non-family friendly: The old folks may struggle if they're on sticks, but daring kids will love it.

Sensory Details

Sights: Sheer cliffs with such a tiny metal pathway along the edge, it hardly seems real, but looks frightening enough to set the heart racing.

Smells: The smell of fear from being so high up, sweaty tourists, sweet tang of energy drinks, the whiff of damp socks.

Taste: The coppery taste of blood if you bite your tongue in fear, bitter after-taste of energy drinks to keep you going.

Touch: The smooth cold feel of metal when you hang on the railings. Or the rough, stony sensation of the rock wall.

Sounds: Hawks squawking, tourists chatting, heavy thumping of boots on metal.

Now Your Turn

Any genre could be staged from high up, or low down for that matter, it just takes imagination and a sprinkling of the details mentioned above, along with your character's dynamic personality to bring the setting alive. Let's see if any of these appeal to you.

The Ultimate Cliffhanger

Name: Preacher's Pulpit

Geographical Area: Preikestolen, Norway

Brief Description: This rocky plateau towers 604 metres above the waters of Lysefjord and juts out dramatically above the spectacular precipice of Preikestolen in Ryfylke. Formed during the Ice Age about 10,000 years ago, when the edges of a glacier bumped up against the surrounding mountains, water from the glacier penetrated the crevices and froze, eventually breaking off colossal portions. Left behind was the dramatic precipice of Preikestolen.

USP: Clearly this is the perfect setting for any mythic story or fantasy. Geologists say that the cracks in the plateau will eventually expand and fragment Pulpit Rock into a pile of rubble. Maybe your character is up there hiking and picnicking with friends when this happens. If so, how will they escape? Maybe one of the group wants to prove himself and accidently falls to his death. Or is pushed, and the friends have to find a way to make it look like an accident.

Floating Mountains

Name: The Tianzi Mountains

Geographical Area: China

Brief Description: Found in the northwest of the Hunan Province in China, these staggering limestone pinnacles are covered in lush greenery and often shrouded in mist. A cable car goes as far as Huangshi village and from here there are plenty of trails to take in the breathtaking views of Tianzi. It's no wonder this amazing place was the inspiration for the floating mountains in the blockbuster movie Avatar.

USP: This location is perfect for a fantasy world. So much so that I having loads of ideas whizzing through my brain as I write this. I am imagining people living here and the things they get up to. Hold on, maybe that's my next novel. Keep in touch with me to find out what happens to this imaginative place.

Suspended Boulder

Name: Kjerag Mountain

Geographical Area: Rogaland, Norway

Brief Description: Suspended high above a huge glacial deposit over a 984-metre-deep abyss, and wedged in the mountain's crevasse, Kjerag is popular with tourists who don't need any climbing equipment and a favourite base jumping site. After several ice ages in Scandinavia, Norway was completely covered in glaciers. Between the ice ages, the meltwater formed the valley. Then global warming caused a rise in sea level, flooding the fjords. This incredibly balanced boulder was apparently deposited during the last glacial period, which wedged the rock into its current position.

USP: Your character could be a modern alien in the form of a human come to check on the status of their 'special stone.' Why the aliens left it there and made humans believe in ice ages is up to your storyline.

Lioness Stalk

Name: Lions Head, SA

Geographical Area: Cape Town, South Africa

Brief Description: Peaking at 669 metres above sea level, Lion's Head stands proud between Table Mountain and Signal Hill. Lion's Head is best known for its stunning views of the Mother City and Table Bay on one side, and the Atlantic shoreline on the other, which makes the hour-long walk to the top really worth the effort. During the 17th century, Dutch settlers first named the peak Leeuwen Kop (Lion's Head). Its counterpart, Signal Hill, was referred to as the Lion's Tail, because the space between the two mountains is reminiscent of a crouching feline.

USP: Because Lions Head is a full of hikers to watch the views over Cape Town, will your character add a little atmosphere by tackling it during full moon and being rewarded with a glittering view of Cape Town by night? Will he meet the love of his life on a balmy summer's evening? Or is he into extreme sports and decides to go paragliding, hang-gliding or micro-lighting instead of a taking romantic walk?

Victorian Monsters

Name: Victoria Falls

Geographical Area: Zimbabwe

Brief Description: Victoria Falls is a town in the province of Matabeleland North, Zimbabwe. It lies on the southern bank of the Zambezi River at the western end of the Victoria Falls. Way back in 1901 the settlement began when the possibility of using the waterfall for hydro-electric power was explored. It expanded when the railway from Bulawayo reached the town shortly before the Victoria Falls Bridge was opened in April 1905, connecting Zimbabwe to what is now Zambia. It became the principal tourism centre for the Falls, experiencing economic booms from mid-nineties.

USP: Is your character a terrorist or war criminal who takes over the area? Or is he the hero who saves the day? Maybe he's simply a dad trying to save his kids from being eaten by the crocs that look like logs in the shallows of the river. I say this because I was on holiday in Rhodesia in its heyday, and watched a horrific accident where a child ran across a 'tumbling log' only to discover it was a predator. Thankfully, it wasn't the size of the one in Lake Placid, but your whacky character may be breeding these monsters?

6 Prominent Panoramas, How Many Others?

Don't limit your character's career, their personality traits or plot events to being adventurous. Instead, make her terrified of heights for these high places. Even if you don't want an adventure romp, give her a new 'best-all-time' job interview in the tallest building in the city. Or give her claustrophobia when she has to take a lift to the manager's office.

I once worked with a girl who walked up 15 stories to join the office team for a Christmas lunch because she wouldn't step into an escalator. Needless to say, the young apprentice who arranged the fancy restaurant, didn't eat much when she found out about her booboo.

More Setting Ideas

Why not attempt some of these ideas? Mountain slopes or sheer edges, a balcony or roof top, in an aeroplane or helicopter, dangling out of a hot air balloon, riding a hang-glider, hiking the steep steps of a tower, cleaning a steeple or rescuing a kitten from a tree top.

Another idea for a high ride is the Millennium Wheel in London. Your character will have to stay put for a while because it's slow as it goes around, but each point gives a stunning view over London.

Or how about having your character come unstuck on a cable car? Or he could be working on the cables and fall in love with a tourist.

Maybe he spots a murder taking place in a cable car going up and he has to rush to find the beautiful yet deadly murderer before she gets away.

There are so many cable cars going up different mountains overlooking stunning settings, like snow peaks in the Alps or sandy beaches in Benalmadena, Spain which takes you on a fifteen-minute ride from the Benalmadena Costa to the summit of Mt. Calamorro, offering spectacular views of the Costa del Sol. Cape Town in South African has an amazing cable car that swivels around slowly as it goes up to Table Mountain so you get the full view. That can be pretty disorientating for nervous characters, and possibly make them giddy or 'sea-sick'.

If you haven't been on a cable car, try looking for a tourist video on YouTube to get the full experience. Depending on your storyline and character's weaknesses, you could try any number of cable cars around the world if you want your hero to take risks on a high ride.

Whether you're writing polar opposites, from romance to murder, the Eiffel Tower in Paris is spectacular for any story taking place ' up high'.

Wide Open Spaces

Forests or canyons are great for when your character is on the run, and can be the perfect place for them.

Untouched Gorge

Name: Verdon Gorge

Geographical Area: France

Brief Description: It is about 25 kilometres long and up to 700 metres deep. The most impressive part lies between the towns of Castellane and Moustiers-Sainte-Marie, where the river has cut a ravine to a depth of seven hundred metres through the limestone mass.

USP: The canyon was formed by the Verdon River, which is named for its startling turquoise-green colour, one of the location's distinguishing characteristics. An adventure would see your character exploring the valleys and ravines.

Mood Details

Mood: Light and peaceful.

Colours: The green in the forest is beautifully mingled with the grey of the rocks, but what stands out is the aquamarine colour of the river which forms this extensive and stunning canyon.

Weather: Sunny, light with varying conditions.

Visual: The cobalt colour of the river is a distinguishing feature of the canyon.

Simile or Metaphor: The canyon looks like a fountain of life, offering tourists an unforgettable experience of olive green hillsides, alabaster cliffs and wide open space.

Item Details

Ground: Rock and stone with numerous hiking trails and dirt tracks, ideal for a European adventure.

Ceiling: Most of the peaks are covered in vegetation.

Walls: The white limestone walls, which are several metres high, attract numerous rock climbers and hikers.

Doors: The caves in the canyon do not have doors, but one still has to be careful when entering this wild, Jurassic gorge. Who knows what creatures could be lurking in the shadows?

Props: Rocks are the primary objects which can be used in this setting. Also, medicinal plants in this area can help a hero in some circumstances.

Obstacles: Nature is an obstacle itself, if your POV doesn't proceed with caution. From slipping from the top of a cliff, to running into a wild animal while hiking, the canyon poses a threat at every turn. Or the mysterious creatures mentioned above.

Plants: The forests flourish with Scots pine and boxwood. The flora is rich with juniper, hawthorn, yarrow and common yarrow to lavender, lily, sage, thyme and rosemary.

Animals: The river is brimming with fish such as trout, carp, barbell, roach, pike... could any of these turn into monsters that frighten your characters, modern or medieval? The Verdon, as a Regional and Natural Park, is a home for chamois, deer, roe deer and wild boar.

It's famous for birds like the griffon vulture and bearded vultures. Your character will find many reptiles, vipers, snakes and lizards. And there may also be small black scorpions. Lots of naturally terrible creatures for a horror story or action adventure, never mind that this is an ideal setting to create a fantasy world similar to that of Jurassic Park. Or have aliens landing here and planning to take over Paris, which is not far away.

General Details

Backstory: The gorge was already described in printed form from 1782 if you fancy this as a historical setting. By the second half of the 19th century, it was featured in French tourist guides.

Genre or Type of Scene: Romance, horror, fantasy, action adventure, love scene, science fiction, young adult or children's adventure.

People details

People: Because of its proximity to the French Riviera, the gorge is very popular with tourists, who can drive around its rim, rent kayaks to travel on the river, or hike. People of different cultures come together to visit one of the most beautiful sites in Europe. They are stepping out of the daily routine and enjoying the beauty of nature.

Family/non-family friendly: Family friendly if your characters can stop the kids poking under every rock and teasing each other with creepy-crawlies. Maybe that's the plot, until one gets bitten or they find a giant alien scorpion. Yuck, I must stop making this stuff up. I'm frightening myself!

Sensory Details

Sights: The shadowy limestone canyon walls are stark against the sparkling turquoise river.

Smells: The smell of clean, crisp air mingles with the strong scents of vegetation and herb, along with the pine-needle waft of the Scots Pine.

Taste: The rich herbal life growing in the valley will delight any outdoor chef with a heady variety of aromas and pleasantly pungent tastes, such as sickly sweet honey combs or the gamy aftertaste of fresh river fish.

Touch: After climbing down a steep abrasive path, your hero may feel a flow of energy shoot through his body when he slides into the chilled water.

Sounds: The sound of birds tweeting above the canyon and crickets in the forests are predominant, along with the rustle of fallen leaves and the crack of branches underfoot.

Other Notes

If you're writing a drama or romance maybe your heroine has Agoraphobia. Triggers for this anxiety may include wide-open spaces or crowds.

Determined to 'woman-up' she joins a hike because she has the hots for the guide. During the hike, and fearing the onset of another panic attack, she realises she has taken on more than she can handle. How will she get through the full hiking program? And still try to impress the 'hottie'?

The wonder of this gorge will fascinate your hero and set him alight with energy and vitality. Leaving all his stress and strain behind, he may hike deeper into the wilds of the gorge.

But we all know we cannot give the hero a happy time-out here (even if we are writing a romance); we must have lots of conflict to keep our readers turning the pages.

Just when your hero freshens up, lifts his mood and relieves his stress … wham! What happens to him? Is it the horrors the kids pull out from under rocks that topple his world? Or those aliens marching on Paris?

Now Your Turn

Wide open spaces beg for a tale of action and adventure that spans across country borders, running into high and low lands. But you don't have to stop there. Why not run your crime thriller through a wide open space? Or a horror where the strange people you create target your group of biologists, geologists or scientists.

Stylish Farmhouse

Name: Country Estate

Geographical Area: Guildford, Surrey

Brief Description: This 40-acre country estate with farmhouse, old beamed cottage, large barn, gym, outdoor pool, beautiful stable block, 10 acre woods, rolling fields with horses could be a lovely setting for a mystery or crime to unfold. Or maybe a classic romance.

USP: Lots of outbuildings that feature country styles for your romance characters to tempt their potential loved one. Maybe turn the estate into a historical setting.

Glamo Woods

Name: Forest Glamping

Geographical Area: East Grinstead, West Sussex

Brief Description: This remote camping site has a wood fire clay oven where evidence of your crime scene could be found. Or you could have a victim drowned in the forest pond. Lots of inspiration for a crime or mystery thriller here, but at the same time your romantic character could be a loner who's disturbed when someone comes camping and lights a fire. Or swing around the location and have this Glamping on an orange grove in Spain, where the heroine comes to pick oranges for summer and meets Mr. Glamping himself!

USP: Strange things could go on in this forest, from supernatural landings to space creatures being bred, to criminal minds hiding bodies. But then, you could also have a sweet romance taking place between camping friends.

Greatest Wildlife Spectacle

Name: Humpback Whale Watching

Geographical Area: Alaska

Brief Description: Arguably the best place in the world for watching whales. With a huge variety of friendly grey whales in their breeding lagoons on the Pacific coast and singing humpback whales off the southern tip, your Marine Biologist heroine would not be a fish out of water.

USP: Peaceful and calm setting for toppling your character out of a boat. Whether their own, as a boat captain guide or a Marine Biologist sent to write the lyrics of singing whales, anything can go wrong in this right place.

Reach for The Sky

Name: Mount Kilimanjaro

Geographical Area: Tanzania

Brief Description: Despite the fact that Mount Kilimanjaro is known as the "Roof of Africa" because it reaches almost twenty thousand feet into the sky as Africa's highest peak, unsurprisingly thousands of people climb it each year. They go through five different climatic zones to reach the summit and take five to ten days to complete.

USP: Your romantic couple may struggle in this setting, but your adventurous, swash-buckling hero would probably foil any bad eggs that get tossed at him in your adventure thriller.

Mountain Crossing

Name: Mont Blanc Massif

Geographical Area: Switzerland, Italy and France

Brief Description: Passing through three countries, this 105-mile hiking trail is one of the world's most popular long-distance routes.

USP: Your hero may think he has just embarked on a simple holiday on the Tour du Mont Blanc. But he has no idea he is about to rescue a whole secluded village from a maniac storm which results in the world's worst snowfalls burying many of the villagers alive.

Divers Paradise

Name: Gardens of the Queen National Park

Geographical Area: Cuba

Brief Description: The Gardens of the Queen National Park is an archipelago of 250 coral and mangrove islands, located 60 miles off Cuba's southern coast, which Fidel Castro established as a marine-protected area and a no-take fishing zone.

USP: Only 1,000 divers are allowed each year, so while your adventurous couple or group of friends plan to see whale sharks, sperm whales, sea turtles, goliath groupers, and some of the most pristine coral reefs anywhere on the planet, they could also witness the greatest undersea treasure hunt taking place right in front of their eyes. Do they try and stop the baddie from killing more divers? Or will they steal the treasure and make a run for it, knowing it could harvest the highest values ever found?

7 Spacious Canvases, and Counting

All you need do is look up American States, Africa, European Continental cities or vistas in New Zealand and Australia. Or how about a vast landscape like Yellowstone National Park?

Maybe try out an area in a completely different part of the world, with the Namaqualand Flower Route. In fact, all the globe's continents will work. And of course, you can use one of the wonders of the world. Or try searching 'tours' + the country where your story takes place.

Your character may be on the hunt for the world's rarest flower and find it five hours north of Cape Town.

Here she'll witness Mother Nature at her proudest when spring flowers suddenly (after a few spots or rain) spring forth in shafts of colour. For a couple of months this 30,000-hectare carpet of vibrant flower heads covers the sandy slopes and rocky sandstone flats of the West Coast National Park.

More Setting Ideas

You could also go for one of these places: Park, beach, open plain, canyon, field or meadow, endless grasslands, desert, ocean, cottage in middle of nowhere or even outer space!

Location, Location, Location

"You can design and create, and build the most wonderful place in the world. But it takes people to make the dream a reality."

Walt Disney

What is a bad location versus a good location? In real estate, it's repeated three times for emphasis, and also so we'll remember the phrase. Mostly, it emphasises the location of a property in determining its value. While this phrase has become a cliché, its meaning still holds true: Location is the most important factor in a home's value.

Okay, so location may not be *the* most important aspect to your entire story, but it is one of the elements that glues your scenes together. (Read CS Lakin's *12 Pillars of Novel Construction* to find out how to cement your novel's entire building structure together).

If you use any of the settings in this book, please do let me know and I will feature your book and the storyline inspired by the setting found here when I update this book with new settings.

If you're on my mailing list, you will get a free copy of any updates. As a reminder here is my Pinterest Scene Settings board: http://bit.ly/21JDdLg.

Settings Can Make or Break a Scene

When I am writing, I have my own Scene Checklist, which has different aspects of creating each and every scene I write about.

I use my Scene Checklist as a kick-start, and then I come back to it at the end to boot my scenes back into a tight order. I have compiled this Checklist organically, as I have read and absorbed much of the awesome advice from the books I have listed. If you'd like to borrow this, you can download my document and use it to create your scenes, or start adding your own checkpoints as well. Download my Scenes Checklist here: http://eepurl.com/bC_vjX

If you download this Scene Checklist and decide to stay on my mailing list, I will send you a free copy of the updated version of *Pimp My Fiction*, which will feature the new books I read and review. Of course if I find any other great resources I will include those too.

When you go to this link you will get the following documents in Word that you can use to create your story structure:

1. Michael Hauge's inner and outer journey diagram
2. His explanation to the six stages to a well-structured story
3. A basic outline of Nigel Watt's eight-point story arc
4. My infographic on writing a thriller
5. My Scene Checklist
6. Scene Settings Checklist

Find all these great resources here: http://eepurl.com/bC_vjX

Aspiring novelists (me included) need to understand what is the most important thing to consider when creating a scene setting.

Authors' Settings Advice

As we're near the end of *101 Writers' Scene Settings* I wanted to end on a high note. So I asked some successful authors and writing tutors what they consider to be the most important considerations when creating a scene setting.

Here's what they said:

Linda Abbott

"I take into account who the character is and their role in the story. The setting is a way to reflect a character's likes or dislikes, allowing the reader a glimpse inside a character's mind which in turn may help to explain their motivation."

Steve Alcorn

"Setting is actually one of your most powerful tools for conveying emotion. How so? Well, setting helps establish the mood of your story. Also, setting can reinforce the theme of your story. Finally, a well-constructed, carefully researched setting helps immerse your reader in the story, which makes all your other words more memorable.

You may draw your characters vividly and create honest and convincing dialogue for them, but without a tangible setting, they'll just be floating in time and space. A well-constructed setting, though, will help ground them, give them a context, and enhance a feeling of reality."

For an easy way to invigorate your whole manuscript, check out Steve's seven steps to bring your setting to life in Chapter 20 of his book, *How to Fix Your Novel.*

James Becker

"I always try to employ a kind of filmic or cinematic technique when describing a location, trying to see it as if through the lens of a camera. And the camera sees everything. Then I try to describe it through the eyes of one or more of the characters, making the reader see – as well as hear and smell – exactly the same thing. Smell, I think, is almost as important as sight in some contexts, because some places genuinely have a smell all their own, like the Old City in Jerusalem.

Avoid generic descriptions like the plague – and particularly clichés like that. Pick an unusual way of expressing something familiar. Not 'a deep, soft voice' but 'a voice like soft footfalls in the snow.' Try and use an unusual or radical description of a place or person, because that will linger in the mind of the reader for a lot longer."

Glenn Cooper

"When writing historical fiction, you'll go a long way toward hooking the reader if you're a stickler for period research and attention to detail. Strive to make everything accurate--the dialogue, accents, and word choices, the sights and sounds and smells and tastes. Engage every sense. Think like a novelist, of course, but also a cinematographer, set designer, costume maker, and hair stylist. Make a movie inside the reader's head."

Mark City

"My settings are usually familiar places - the home or the office - as I think it's scarier for readers to imagine darkness creeping into their house or place of work.

Having said that, sometimes I introduce a 'bad place,' like a house in the middle of a forest, because that plays on our most primal fears. In *Follow You Home*, the main characters stumble, like Hansel and Gretel, upon such a house. You can learn a lot from fairy tales..."

Dean Crawford

"My most important considerations for setting a scene are those that happen before the reader actually sees the scene. By this I mean *expectation*. I'll often present an approaching scene with a line of dialogue that might be something along the lines of: *'You'll have to see it to believe it...'* and then end the chapter there, forcing the reader to read one more chapter in order to find out what it is they won't believe unless they see it. It's a handy page-turning motivator.

Once in the scene, pace and tension count the most. I never do the reveal too early. It's no good describing the scene in immense detail as readers can get bored, so instead I'll hit the reader once again with dialogue such as: *'Oh my God.'* Then come the main impressions the main character experiences in the first few seconds: major sights, sounds and smells, before I then reveal what it is that they're looking at that's so relevant to the story, be it a body, a clue or whatever.

Expectation, then tension, then pace as the scene's importance to the story is revealed."

Nicole Evelina

"The amount of detail you need to include will vary by genre. For example, historical fiction and sci-fi or fantasy will have more than contemporary fiction because you're introducing your readers to a whole new world. Whether you use a little or a lot of detail, remember the purpose of setting is twofold: 1) to give the reader a sense of where the action takes place, and 2) to convey something about the plot and/ or characters.

The first is pretty self-explanatory, but very necessary. We need to know where we are in each scene because if we don't, wondering about it will take us out of the scene. The second goes to the idea that setting isn't just window dressing; it has purpose. Where you choose to set your scene, the weather, even the wallpaper, can and should be a reflection of or influence on something you are trying to convey.

No matter what type of book you write, it's important to keep your setting descriptions in line with what your POV character would notice. If it's some place new, they will notice more than if it's a place they go all the time. In the same way, if the character is upset, chances are good they are more focused on their inner turmoil than what is going on around them.

What your character does for a living may influence what they notice, as well. For example, an engineer or architect (or an enthusiast in those areas) would notice the details of the way a building is constructed (materials, architectural style, etc.), whereas a nurse might notice the garden out back that contains medicinal herbs, or a mother might see all the sharp edges of a room that could be hazardous to a child."

Jeff Gerke

"Every setting in every scene in your book (and every character too, by the way) must be fully described to the reader. If you're not *seeing* it, the reader sure won't be *seeing* it either.

In other words, if the writer doesn't imagine the setting herself and then render that description on the page, the reader will get a big fat nothing when she tries to imagine what's going on in the scene.

If the writer doesn't describe it, it doesn't exist for the reader. You may be picturing the setting perfectly (although maybe you're not), but if you don't write it down so the reader can peek over your shoulder, she gets zilch in terms of a sense for what's happening and where."

Read Tip #96 at http://bit.ly/1p4oHN3 for Jeff's six components to describe your setting.

CS Lakin

"Settings is one of the most neglected elements with novelists.

Setting should always be filtered through the POV character's senses and not plopped down as merely information given by the author. Setting can be a powerful tool to convey mood, emotion, metaphor, motifs, and tone, so it behooves writers to learn how to convey setting in a thoughtful way for best effect."

Marti Leimbach

"The settings I remember the most are the ones that end up influencing what happens in the novel. For example, in *Going After Cacchiato* by Tim O'Brien, the setting is the war and the war pretty much becomes a character."

Rayne Hall

"Use smells to let the reader experience the place. A single sentence describing odours achieves more than a whole paragraph of visuals. What does the room smell of: Beeswax and patchouli? Boiled cabbage and disinfectant? Pizza and unwashed socks?"

Angela Marsons

"The most important considerations for me when creating a setting for a scene is deciding what I want it to add to the narrative. If it's a crime scene or a dark moment I ask myself how can the setting contribute to the overall mood of the scene I'm trying to create. For a crime scene I might choose a particularly dark alleyway to enhance the sense I'm trying to create."

Allison Maruska

"The most important consideration when setting a scene is including as many sensory details as possible. Sight is a given, but it's also important to include unusual smells, maybe what the air feels like, and if there are background noises."

Alex Myers

"I love settings. What would the TV show "Lost" have been without the island? Could Jack and Rose have been on any other stage than the 'Titanic'?

I think in a lot of cases 'setting' is as important as a main character. Sometimes setting is so important it appears right in the title like *Downton Abbey*, *Alice in Wonderland*, *On the Road* or *The Chronicles of Narnia*.

Where would James Michener have been without his one-word setting titles like Texas, Chesapeake, Alaska or even Space. Give me a good enough setting and I'll remember that scene for the rest of my life. It sounds like *101 Writers' Scene Settings* is a book I'll want to keep right on my writing desk."

Jodie Renner

"Sensory details suck your readers in. In order for your story and characters to come to life on the page, your readers need to be able see what the main character is seeing, hear what he's hearing, and smell, taste and feel along with him. And to empathize with and bond with the character, readers also need to feel her reactions and thoughts. To bring your scene and characters to life and engage the readers, evoke all or most of the five senses in almost every scene.

Details about the setting should always be filtered through the character, never the author butting in to describe or explain things to the readers. The story should be told through your character's viewpoint, as they're moving through that world, observing and reacting to what's going on around them.

So just describe elements your character would be aware of at that moment, and color them with your character's mood, agenda, and personality. Different characters will notice different aspects of their environment, depending on their background, how they're feeling, and what they're looking for or hoping to accomplish. Avoid blandly describing the setting, like a travelogue. Show the setting through the character's viewpoint, with attitude!"

Here's what Jodie says in Chapter 22 of her book *Captivate Your Readers:*

"So if you want to write riveting fiction (and who doesn't?), don't keep your readers at a distance, impassively reading the words on the page. Suck them right into your story world, your fictive dream, by making them feel like they're right there with your character, like they are your character. Evoke sights, sounds, smells, and tastes from the readers' own memory banks, which will trigger emotions. Scents especially bring back feelings and memories which readers can draw upon to be active participants in your story.

And show us what the characters are thinking and feeling, too — their inner and outer reactions to what's going on around them. All of this enhances the readers' experience and deepens their emotional investment with your story."

Douglas E. Richards

"Settings come in so many varieties it is very difficult to generalize. I would say that no matter what, each setting needs to serve the plot well, rather than satisfying the personal whims of the author.

In my latest novel, *Split Second,* I set a scene at USC, but later decided that it would be useful to have my protagonists escape using the steam tunnels that so many universities seem to have. The only problem was that research revealed that USC wasn't one of these universities. So I deleted these pages and moved the setting to UCLA instead, and was able to incorporate elements of real life accounts of journeys through UCLA's extensive tunnels.

Each novel will have dozens of settings. Some will be garden variety: in a restaurant, hotel room, or car, and for these I would argue that less is more. Most people know what the inside of a typical Denny's might look like, so two-page descriptions just slow the story down. Some settings will be more exotic or unfamiliar, and these require research by the author.

It might require reading ten pages on a setting, or a personal visit, to find just a few tidbits to really give readers a sense that they are being given a (brief) tour by an insider.

To take the UCLA example, my research indicated that the university seems to always be in a state of constant building or re-building, so much so that students have decided that UCLA stands for Under Construction Like Always. Sprinkling just a few additions like this can make a setting more interesting and relatable."

Joyce Schneider

"No matter how different any setting is, what's important is how you make it sensory and emotional. The room darkened; the water glinted; the branches flailed; the lab smelled of mice and antiseptic, the tunnel echoed, stormy haze, crippled old house, sudsy tide."

Kevin Wignall

"Don't kill the scene with detail. The reader doesn't need to know the exact location of the furniture in the room, or descriptions of all the stores on the street. Give a brief feel for the setting and let the reader imagine the rest."

Vincent Zandri

"Settings are organically dictated by the plot. After all, the writer goes where the characters need to go. I just got through writing a chapter that took me from the woods, to a farmhouse, to a Jeep, to another farmhouse, to the farmhouse kitchen, and back out to the woods, all within the course of about three or four hundred words. My settings are almost always places I'm familiar with, or have been familiar with at some point in my life.

I'm not the type to Google a setting, but choose instead to go there, which is why I travel so much. Plus, it's good to get out of the house for a while. Even for months at a time."

Now Your Turn

So there you have it. The key to unlock the door to creating vivid and memorable scene settings shown through your character's eyes.

Unlock Your Settings

"When you leave a beautiful place, you carry it with you wherever you go."
Alexandra Stoddard

As I said on the first page of this book, scene settings are critical pieces of the puzzle that will eventually make up your entire novel.

Whether you're looking for inspiration for a new setting or re-examining a current scene location that isn't working, I hope *101 Writers' Scene Settings* has inspired you.

More than that, excite your readers with new places for them to experience through your characters. Let them share your character's travels to new places, so they can meet new people and experience new emotions — through y*our* stories.

There's a brave new world out there. Go out into it. Go forth and conquer your scenes settings.

A world of possibility awaits.

The End of
101 Writers' Scene Settings

If you enjoyed reading *101 Writers' Scene Settings*, please take a moment to share your thoughts with a review on Amazon, Goodreads, Smashwords, Kobo, Nook or iBooks. It doesn't have to be glowing, only genuine and fair. All you need to do is click the review link on this book's page. Thank you for your support!

Read on for more books by this author, acknowledgements, notes and bonus materials.

Writers' Resource Series

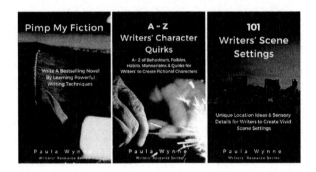

Pimp My Fiction: Write A Bestselling Novel By Learning Powerful Writing Techniques

&

A~Z Writers' Character Quirks: Writers' A~Z of Behaviours, Foibles, Habits, Mannerisms & Quirks for Writers to Create Fictional Characters

&

101 Writers' Scene Settings: Unique Location Ideas & Sensory Details for Writers to Create Vivid Scene Settings

Check for future editions: http://paulawynne.com/writers-resource-series

Bonus Material

1. Don't forget to download Scene Settings Checklist:
   http://eepurl.com/bC_vjX

2. Remember to pick up your FREE copy of *Pimp My Fiction*:
   http://eepurl.com/bC336f

3. Join Paula Wynne's mailing list to receive the latest news about upcoming releases and specials just for subscribers:
   http://eepurl.com/byjPVT

If you stay on Paula's mailing list, you will be given the opportunity to get a free review copy of her next books.

4. Scenes Checklist: Download Paula's Scenes Checklist to create your scenes:
   http://eepurl.com/bC_vjX

5. Free sample chapters of *Pimp My Site, The Grotto's Secret* and *A~Z Writers' Character Quirks*:
   http://eepurl.com/byv2wT

With the Checklists you'll be added to my mailing list and I will send you free copies of future updates.

Acknowledgements

A big thanks to my beta reader Ros Brookman, who always gives me excellent feedback and advice, along with some extra settings ideas.

I would like to express my gratitude to the authors who have shared their best advice on how to create vivid settings:

Linda Abbott, Steve Alcorn, James Becker, Glenn Cooper, Mark City, Dean Crawford, Nicole Evelina, Jeff Gerke, CS Lakin, Marti Leimbach, Rayne Hall, Angela Marsons, Allison Maruska, Alex Myers, Jodie Renner, Douglas E. Richards, Joyce Schneider, Kevin Wignall and Vincent Zandri.

About The Author

As an award-winning entrepreneur Paula Wynne has appeared on TV several times, including breakfast shows and has been featured in various magazines and national newspapers.

Paula and her husband Ken starred in the BBC Show, *Escape to the Continent*, which showed their quest to live in Spain so Paula could become a full time writer.

For many years Paula has been obsessed with learning everything to improve her writing. She has acquired a bookshelf of excellent reference books by highly acclaimed authors, so she wrote *Pimp My Fiction: Secrets of How to Write a Novel*. This inspired a Writers' Resource Series with *101 Writers' Scene Settings* and *A~Z Writers' Character Quirks*.

Paula received an 'Honourable Mention' in the 75th Annual Writers Digest Writing Competition for two unpublished novels, which inspired her to continue writing.

Now Paula is really excited to be publishing her first novel, *The Grotto's Secret*.

Printed in Great Britain
by Amazon

85400024R00102